Washington Geographic Series

WASHINGTON MOUNTAIN RANGES

BY ROBERT U. STEELQUIST

published by
AMERICAN GEOGRAPHIC PUBLISHING

RICK GRAETZ, PUBLISHER
MARK THOMPSON, DIRECTOR OF PUBLICATIONS
BARBARA FIFER, ASSISTANT BOOK EDITOR

This series provides in-depth information about Washington's geographical, natural history, historical and cultural subjects. Design by Len Visual Design. Printed in Japan by DNP America, Inc., San Francisco.

To Peter

Robert Steelquist's experience in Washington's mountains stems from 25 years of recreational hiking and climbing as well as working as a trailhand and naturalist for the National Park Service. An environmental activist, he has worked with local, state and federal agencies to preserve Washington's natural heritage. Mr. Steelquist is the author of two books on the Olympic Peninsula and director of a marine science center in Port Angeles. He and his family live at the foot of Blyn Mountain, between the Olympic Mountains and the Strait of Juan de Fuca.

Front cover photos, clockwise from left:
Paradise Park and Mt. Rainier. JEFF GNASS
Mt. Anderson and penstemons. PAT O'HARA
Lupine. PAT O'HARA
Little Annapurna with larches. PAT O'HARA
Climbing Mt. Adams at dawn. © GARY BRAASCH

American Geographic Publishing
Box 5630
Helena, Montana 59601
(406) 443-2842
Idaho • Montana • Oregon • Washington • Wyoming

ISBN 0-938314-25-4

Top: Huckleberry leaves amid boulders, Alpine Lakes Wilderness. Bottom: Bunchberry dogwood flowers. PAT O'HARA PHOTOS

Acknowledgments

I owe many thanks to Jenny for her support, her criticism, and for guarding my task of writing. Thanks to Pat O'Hara for his encouragement and critical comments; Gail E.H. Evans for locating and arranging the use of the historical photographs; Karna Orsen for specimen and copy photography; Beverly Steelquist for researching peaks and elevations; and Laurel Black of Anaglyph Art Services for map and illustration art.

Ron Crawford of Peninsula College; Jerry Hickman, Washington Department of Game; Mike Scott, Idaho Fish and Game; Hank Warren, Bill Dengler, John Douglass and Ed Schreiner, all of the National Park Service, read chapters and provided valuable comments. Nelsa Buckingham; Mark Sheehan, Washington Natural Heritage Program; and Ed Alvorsen assisted with botanical information. Carolyn Dreidger, U.S. Geologic Survey, made valuable suggestions about glaciology. Don Hyndman, University of Montana, provided helpful insight into terrane and geosyncline theories.

Quotations attributed to Calder Bressler originally appeared in Harvey Manning's article "Ptarmigans and Their Ptrips," *The Mountaineer*. They are reprinted with the permission of the Mountaineers. Quotations from Joann Roe, taken from her book, *The North Cascadians* were reprinted with the permission of Madrona Publishers, Seattle, Washington.

Fossil specimens photographed for the book were provided through the courtesy of the Geology and Paleontology Division of the Thomas Burke Memorial Washington State Museum, University of Washington. The photograph of Louis Henderson was made available by Jean and Walter Walkinshaw. Photographs appearing in the section on Barron, Washington, were provided by Jack Harris, of Twisp, Washington, with reprints courtesy of John Andrist. The map of the Slate Creek Mining District is based upon material provided by The Shorey Bookstore, Seattle.

Special thanks go to my mountain companions through the years: My brothers, Paul, Mark, Dan and Tim; the Ayer brothers, the Stata brothers and Doug French; the Happy Trails crews; Olympic National Park crews; Tom Sullivan for geology rambles, November footlogs and dynamite; my father, Davis Steelquist, who turned me toward mountains and let me go.

View from Indian Henry's Hunting Ground, Mt. Rainier National Park. PAT O'HARA

Washington Mountain Ranges

Contents

Introduction 6

CHAPTER ONE
Mountain Building 16

CHAPTER TWO
Mountain Carving 26

CHAPTER THREE
Life of Mountains 38

CHAPTER FOUR
The Old Continental Ranges 48

CHAPTER FIVE
Okanogan Country 54

CHAPTER SIX
The Cascades 62

CHAPTER SEVEN
The Olympics 74

CHAPTER EIGHT
The Young Volcanics 82

Washington's 50 Tallest Peaks 100

References 101

Soleduck River, Olympic National Park. PAT O'HARA

"In various travels and expeditions in the territory, I had viewed the snow peaks of this range from all points of the compass, and since that time have visited the mountain regions of Europe, and most of those of North America, I assert that Washington Territory contains mountain scenery in quantity and quality sufficient to make half a dozen Switzerlands..."

Lieutenant August Valentine Kautz, U.S. Army, 1875

Sunset from Deer Park, Olympic National Park. PAT O'HARA

INTRODUCTION

Western bluebird. TOM & PAT LEESON

Daylight reaches Mt. Rainier (14,410'), Washington's highest summit. PAT O'HARA

The mention of Washington State evokes an admixture of landform images—dusty, rolling hills of the Palouse, seastacks and crushing breakers of the Pacific coastline, mist-shrouded lowland forests, and rock strewn steppes of the coulee country. But more than any of these, there is the image of mountains—cool heights; serene snow-caps; walls of variegated rock rising out of dark forests—all of which characterize Washington's many ranges. Rising in the distance over the state's plains and lowlands, Washington's mountain ranges challenge our sensibilities. They bewilder our sense of orderly domination over land. They alternately perplex our sense of direction and guide us as if they are magnetic lodes to our compass eye. They form in us a peculiar companionship with land, the absence of which creates the awesome loneliness one mountain-bred feels on open prairie.

Indeed, as one who grew up within sight of the Cascades and later endured the emptiness of midwestern horizons, I find that it is the vision of summits and shoulders, notches and tarns, lake basins and sedge-filled meadows that characterizes Washington for me. It is the comfort of closeness that endears mountains to me—a world of bounds. It is the confidence in a distant snow line that guides my selection of a jacket as I leave home. It is the warmth of alpenglow with which I judge the beauty of a sunset. It has been on the slopes and summits of mountains that I have best understood myself.

Mountains can be considered as irregularities of the earth's surface, ripples on an otherwise taut skin. They are volumes of rock heaped upon or extruded out of a planet that seeks to be uniformly round. They are the roots of old volcanoes and layers of archaic sediments crumbling under various weathers, returning to new seas. In the slow dance of continents, they are the products of nudgings. They are the upshot of crustal plates that go bump in the night of eons. They are the reefs of ancient seas, the shores of once-distant islands stranded along an old continental shore. They are places where the unbelievable forces harnessed within the planet find their way out.

Mountains are also wrinkles of other sorts. They represent intrusions of the arctic into temperate latitudes; there is a remarkable corollary between feet of elevation gained on a mountain slope and miles traveled toward the Arctic Circle. Looking down on the northern hemisphere from a theoretical point over the Pole, we would see lines representing temperature gradients looping southward along the fronts of the continental mountain ranges, sometimes perpendicular to the even circles of latitude.

They also curve time, altering seasons and cycles. Winter, broken for nine months at low elevations, lingers for nine in high country. The vernal bloom of the lowland has long finished before flowers of the same species brighten a subalpine meadow.

The mountains form a window through which we look 10,000 years into the past. Only here can we catch glimpses of the remnant populations of Pleistocene mammals like the hairy white antelope we call the mountain goat and relict cave bears now known as grizzly. Only in the tundra patches and forests of remote mountains of northeastern Washington do caribou continue to hold onto a minute vestige of the Ice Age. And it is mountains that hold the scattered shards remaining of the glaciers that once sheeted the continent.

Mountains contain perhaps one of Washington's most significant keys to its past—the wild itself. Overlooked in the settlement boom that peopled the lowlands with

Top: A caravan of hardy motorists pause en route to Mt. Baker beneath the picturesque form of Mt. Shuksan. COURTESY UNIVERSITY OF WASHINGTON
Bottom: Washington's mountains are composed of various materials—some formed in the earth's fiery mantle, others in the cool beds of ancient oceans. KARNA ORSEN

Mountain landforms—tilted beds, glacier-carved lake basins, distant snowcaps—establish a distinctive environment both close and familiar to most Washingtonians. Here are Lake Angeles and Mt. Baker.
PAT O'HARA

Euro-Americans, much of mountain country defied permanent settlement. Fragments endured the mining of ore, the cutting of timber and the impulse to civilize. Today it is the mountainous areas of the state that are preserved as wilderness areas, national parks and monuments. Patches of pre-settlement landscape sprawl beneath the peaks of Washington's loftiest mountains, and although metropolitan areas are identifiable by their man-caused haze, the sea of peaks receding over the curving horizon imparts an abiding humility. Ironically, land once considered unfit for people has become a rare and cherished resource for the modern soul.

Washington State is often thought of as having two sides; a wet side and a dry side. Mountains divide the two and mountain passes form the agreed-upon boundaries. Mountains even create the climatic variation that gives rise to the distinction. Yet, for all of its simple beauty, the two-side theory does little justice to the variety of mountain terrain found in all parts of the state. What is overlooked in such a picture is the remarkable diversity of Washington's mountainscapes—diversity of origins, age, and substance as well as diversity of what mountains affect—weather, soils, plant and animal communities, and the perpetual cycle of running water.

This book is intended to illuminate some of that diversity. It is meant to teach what the mountain ranges themselves can teach—lessons in the evolution of plants and animals, the distribution of human settlement, the rise and fall of landforms, and the shaping of continents. The book is not intended as a textbook on mountain geology, nor a road guide, but rather a description, an interpretation, of Washington's dominant topographic features. Its focus is not the conquest of peaks nor the tracery of footpaths that connect the Washington's mountain world to civilization. The challenge of the ranges lies instead in their power to broaden our wisdom—intellectually and spiritually. They are keys to unlock the ages, that we may experience our short lives in the context of the slow transformation of the earth. As Theodore Winthrop, an adventuresome easterner who crossed the Cascades in 1853, wrote after seeing Mount Rainier, "The noble works of nature, and mountains most of all, have power to make Our noisy years seem moments in the being Of the eternal silence'."

Washington's mountains endure, yet they are not changeless. They live, rise, erode, react and act upon. Occasionally, they explode. They form a stage, upon which we play our scene. They form the backdrop against which we see what is near.

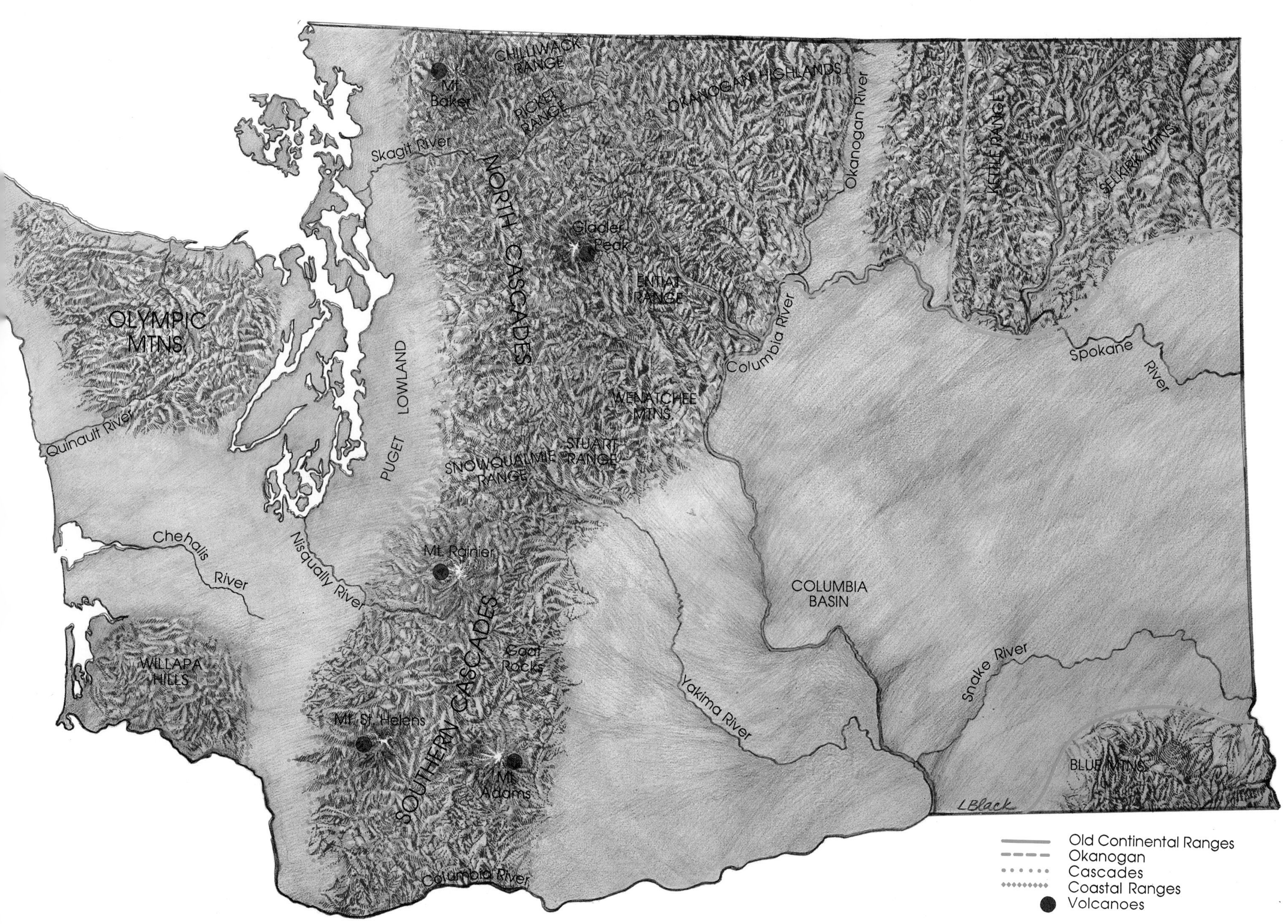
CHILLIWACK RANGE
Mt. Baker
PICKET RANGE
OKANOGAN HIGHLANDS
Okanogan River
KETTLE RANGE
SELKIRK MTNS.
Skagit River
NORTH CASCADES
Glacier Peak
ENTIAT RANGE
OLYMPIC MTNS.
Columbia River
Spokane River
PUGET LOWLAND
WENATCHEE MTNS.
Quinault River
STUART RANGE
SNOWQUALMIE RANGE
Chehalis River
Nisqually River
Mt. Rainier
COLUMBIA BASIN
SOUTHERN CASCADES
Goat Rocks
WILLAPA HILLS
Yakima River
Snake River
Mt. St. Helens
Mt. Adams
BLUE MTNS.
LBlack
Columbia River
Old Continental Ranges
Okanogan
Cascades
Coastal Ranges
Volcanoes

Wild rhododendron (above), Washington's state flower, thrives in conifer forests of western Washington's mountain foothills and lowlands. The juxtaposition of the wild and cultivated is a prime characteristic of the Washington landscape. Skagit Valley daffodils (right), raised in rich alluvial soil and rainwater that are gifts of the nearby Cascades, will announce the arrival of spring on city street corners of Europe and North America. PAT O'HARA PHOTOS

Mountains and People

It was John Meares who named the coastal Olympus. George Vancouver named the big western Cascades. Both navigators had come off the smooth roundness of the world's ocean and toward a land jagged at daybreak with the crests of a sea of peaks. The impression was pronounced. The naturalist aboard Vancouver's sloop *Discovery*, Archibald Menzies wrote, "... the low land at the head of the Bay swelled out very gradually to form a most beautiful & majestic Mountain of great elevation whose line of ascent appeard [*sic*] equally smooth & gradual on very side with a round obtuse summit coverd two thirds of its height down with perpetual Snow as were also the summits of a rugged ridge of Mountains that proceeded from it to the Northward." He was describing Mt. Rainier—an image as fresh today as then.

For others, particularly those who settled during the middle third of the 19th century, mountains were landscapes of promise, for they announced the nearness of the Zions of the Northwest. Broad fertile plains, tumbling rivers, abundant rainfall and plenty of land lay at the feet of the cool heights. Pioneer writer Phoebe Goodell Judson painted a picture in her 1925 book of frontier recollection *A Pioneer's Search for an Ideal Home,* "It was one of Washington's lovliest October days, brightened by the snow-capped peaks of the mountains glistening in the morning sunshine; and the gorgeous hues of the maple foliage on the low lands, with a background of the ever green fir and cedar, presenting a landscape refreshing to the souls of the weary emigrants." Clearly, mountains formed the backdrop in her personal land of promise.

Through sentiments of hers and others, Washington's mountains, as scenery, made their way into the literature of discovery and natural wonders of the 18th and 19th centuries. In the unwritten and unrecorded lives of soldiers, settlers, goldseekers, roustabouts, teamsters, doctors, midwives and circuit riders, Washington's mountains lent a particular color and formed a dramatic environment for the business of creating a civilization. Isolation and frostbite held even sway in the balance with Manifest Destiny. Civilized places like Monte Cristo and Barron reverted to wild land when ore prices dropped, the veins were exhausted or the wills of their founders softened.

To some, the mountains comprised a useless territory,

Looking up Dumas Street in Monte Cristo in 1894. Rich ore lodes lured thousands of fortune-seekers into Washington's mountains during the first half-century of statehood. Wealth proved elusive and makeshift cities, robbed of the illusions that created them, withered. COURTESY UNIVERSITY OF WASHINGTON

of little enough utility not to warrant the effort needed to subdue the raging mountain freshets, the brittle, rotten rock and the gloomy, sodden forests. Lieutenant Joseph P. O'Neill, fresh from discovering the valley labyrinths of the south-central Olympics, wrote in a report to Congress, "... while the country on the outer slope of these mountains is valuable, the interior is useless for all practical purposes. It would, however, serve admirably for a national park. There are numerous elk—that noble animal so fast disappearing from this country—that should be protected." O'Neill's prophetic words reveal sentiments rare in his era, yet in a time when isolated settlements were still engulfed in a wilderness, "practicality" was an important measure of the worth of land—exploitable resources, and not real estate, were the grist of the frontier economy mill.

In contemporary Washington, mountains are visible and tangible reminders of an out-of-doors close at hand. Our skyscrapers eclipse them as the foreshortening eye superimposes metropolitan skylines over the backlight rose of a winter dawn. Glazed architectural curtain-walls beam sunset reflections to the summits of the Olympics. Washingtonians and Washington visitors flock to the mountains. We hike the guidebooks ragged, we photograph, we wade the mountain rivers, we have made mountains into businesses that manufacture everything from wax-based boot grease to goose-down booties. The

Above: The upper reaches of Cameron Creek, near Lost Pass in the Olympics. PAT O'HARA
Right: A 1907 climbing party atop Mt. Queets in the Olympics. COURTESY WASHINGTON STATE HISTORICAL SOCIETY

"mountain look" has become a standard in fashion, with parkas designed for Washington summits (and named after them) adorning city-bound bodies across the nation.

The reasons are varied, but a single thread connects our multiple fascinations with the mountains. They are direct and elemental. Their thin air cleanses. Their landscapes are sharp in contrast, a pleasant respite from the sprawling uniformity of urban and suburban landscapes. They are squeaky clean, the way the continent was squeaky clean when this land's earliest inhabitants hunted hairy elephants. Technology has equipped us with the most, at the least weight, so we can venture into the mountains as individuals, soft bodies and separate civilizations, so that we can physically and metaphorically confront unadorned relicts of a land we have otherwise subdued. We climb mountains, not as Mallory said, "because they are there," but because we are there, and because there is little else we can do with them.

For the purposes of this book, Washington's ranges are divided into parts that reflect the distinct processes of the formation of the land. Boundaries are not strictly geographic because, as in the case of the Cascades volcanoes, a new range lies over an older range. In this book, Washington's mountainscapes are arranged according to their life-spans, their biological and geomorphic attributes—the things that truly make them separate. The Olympics, for example, are viewed in relation to the Willapa Hills, with whom they share their oceanic origin. The Selkirks and Kettle Range are viewed together for their affinity with the old continent edge. The Cascades are seen as two ranges—one, an older continental mass of volcanic and metamorphic rock, deformed mechanically by compression and marked by great thrust faults; the other, a newer range of isolated volcanoes, active and changing in the era of human habitation.

The book seeks to be non-technical, explaining landscapes in terms that make sense when the reader looks at the land. Its photographs are selected to represent not only physical and biological processes outlined in the text, but to convey the sensation that accompanies the capture of a particular moment, when self-awareness is lost and the eye caresses the textures of the irregular lighted surfaces of the mountainscape. Other resources—reference works, mountaineering organiza-

In mountain landscapes the survival struggle is intensified by extremes in all the factors upon which life itself must depend. Here, tufted saxifrage thrives in the relative protection of a single boulder. PAT O'HARA

Evening light, the aftermath of a storm viewed from Buttermilk Butte in the North Cascades. PAT O'HARA

tions, and agencies that manage the mountain landscapes of Washington—are listed in the appendix. These sources can lead the reader more deeply into particular regions, ideas or activities that are associated with Washington's mountain ranges.

It is my hope that this book conveys the vitality of Washington's mountains, the life-histories not only of the living things they support but also of their rock, ice and thin air. Enduring as the horizon, mountains are themselves symptoms of earthly flux. They represent a precarious delicacy that we too can upset. But treading lightly, we can savor the refuge they provide. We can witness the shape of time they measure, and challenge ourselves to understand.

William O. Douglas

Perhaps no individual has championed the cause of wilderness—as part and parcel of fundamental human rights bestowed by the Constitution—as William O. Douglas.

Douglas was raised in the shadow of Washington's Cascades, where sweet water tumbled out of the mountains to join the Yakima River as it meandered among willow and cottonwoods. The fragrance of ponderosa, sage and woodsmoke and the taste of pale trout flesh were deeply embedded in his young identity. An early childhood bout with infantile paralysis never let him take for granted the gift of vigor—painful hikes into the mountain country healed him.

Recollections of boyhood dreams lasted throughout his lifetime, guarded over by the enduring presences of Mt. Adams and Mt. Rainier. His education in the east was as much the education of a painful separation from the snow sentinels of his boyhood as it was studying the writings of classical scholars and great jurists. Throughout his long career as an attorney, judge and Supreme Court Justice, Douglas drew inspiration and strength from mountains and the wilderness they hold.

"Mountains have a decent influence on men," he once wrote, and he devoted much of his life to assuring that significant remnants of mountain wilderness would be preserved. Morality itself was at stake, and as one chosen to stand vigil over the fundamental instruments of morality that our nation has created, Justice Douglas rose to eloquence to argue that even mountains, among other inanimate natural objects, possess certain legal rights.

Douglas witnessed the transformation of the Yakima Valley, its native people, the tributary rivers and their wheatgrass meadows. He also witnessed, over his lifetime, a parallel transformation of the American landscape, from the old Appalachians to the Brooks Range. In that transformation he saw the spectre of monetary greed set upon the land that had nourished and healed him, a land that, by his own prescription, could nourish and heal all persons. He made all the world's mountains his own, but reserved a special affection for Washington's wilderness ranges. In his writings, the Olympics, the Cascades volcanoes, Goat Rocks and the North Cascades showed their hold on him. He recounted youthful misadventures and auspicious companions, always sharing the mark that the mountains and his mountain company left on his thought.

A long and productive career in the Supreme Court gave Douglas ample opportunity to contribute to the betterment of the human condition. Even that, however, is overshadowed by his devotion to the wild and its security. We all are greatly enriched by the visions he shared of a world where cool winds descend the slopes of benign volcano giants and fill our lungs with the refreshment of mountain wilderness.

William O. Douglas (1898-1980)—Associate Justice, U.S. Supreme Court; ardent conservationist. Imbued with a passion for the wild early in his life, Douglas often returned to Washington's mountains, which he once called "hallowed country, where one walks softly." PHOTOS COURTESY YAKIMA VALLEY MUSEUM

Above: Dewey Lake, Cougar Lakes area of the Cascades in the William O. Douglas Wilderness. PAT O'HARA

CHAPTER ONE

MOUNTAIN BUILDING

KARNA ORSEN

"Mount St. Helens Erupting," oil by Paul Kane, 1847. Kane based his painting on eyewitness accounts of an 1842 eruption.
COURTESY ROYAL ONTARIO MUSEUM, TORONTO, ONTARIO, CANADA

Across a deep blue gulf of mountain air the ridges are falling into shadow. Where flat rays of sunlight break through the mountains from the west, the peaks glow. The light weakens and the shadows advance. Steep ravines spill their darkness. The mountain shapes, the layered strata, the talus, quickly lose their form in the even shade. Suddenly the light has gone and with it, heat. A particular quiet—a coolness—climbs the last easy slope to catch me on the crest. A transformation has completed itself. A day is over. An instant of mountain time passes and, save the clatter of a slight rockfall, loosed by a misplaced hoof or paw, these mountains have not changed. The hanging stillness seems like the idea of eternity itself. In all honesty, I cannot explain, from experience, how these mountains got here or what they will yet become.

It is common to link dissimilar processes together, even if only in metaphor, in order to illustrate things that our lives otherwise would not inform us about. The birth of mountains is such a process. We could give them personalities, give them lifespans of infancy, youth, and age. Myths—western, eastern and otherwise—have served that purpose. We could give them abrupt beginnings, to characterize their building as a constructive act by some person-like being. Yet somehow, the fivescore years that limit all but a few human lifespans are lost in the time it takes a mountain to rise and fall in the cycle of its own lifespan. In that timeframe, human beings could, or could not, have emerged as life-forms on our planet and no difference would be pronounced.

The process by which mountains form is called "orogenesis," Greek for "mountain birth." We call a general mountain-building era an "orogeny." Thus, we give even the production of mountains a familiar and organic name, one that metaphorically links earthly processes to our own.

Washington's mountain ranges vividly portray many of the ways that mountains are formed. Volcanic processes belch forth, creating our dominant peaks. The snowy domes of Mt. Rainier, Mt. Baker, Glacier Peak, Mt. Adams and the headless Mt. St. Helens are all very recent additions to the Washington mountainscape and represent a modern episode of volcanism.

Some volcanic activity remains smothered, creating blisters that expose their filling only after eons of erosion. The Stuart Range is a classic example of the erosion-resistant remains of a massive injection of magma that saw the light of day only after the surrounding rock weathered and was carried away by glaciers and running water.

Fluid motions of the earth's crust give the continents the graceful mobility of a corps de ballet. Wide-ranging currents in the earth's mantle have carried distant island arcs and ocean plateaus thousands of miles, implanting exotic rock along ancient continental margins. Parts of the Okanogan Highlands are thought to be the fragments of an island mini-continent, plastered onto the old edge of North America approximately 100 million years ago.

Not all movement in the earth is as spectacular. Throughout Washington's mountains are signs of more localized motion—faults revealing movement of dozens of feet, as well as faults that reveal displacement of tens of miles.

Alpine larch and Prusik Peak, Enchantment Basin. A deeply eroded dome of granite, the Stuart Range consists of magma that cooled far beneath the earth's surface and was exposed when the overlying country eroded away.
PAT O'HARA

The buoyancy of the continent is displayed in formations that have risen from the earth's interior where they were combined, cooked, pressed—metamorphosed into dark, streaky puddings. Old seabed, still bearing the fossilized remains of its living communities, has been hoisted onto the shoulders of the land; fossil clamshells form alpine rockeries that bloom with penstemon and harebells.

Our understanding of our mountains forms an important yardstick of the achievement of human imagination as it answers the major questions about the nature of our planet. Like distant orogenies themselves, epochs of

This page, top: Many of Washington's mountains consist of sandstones and shales, the sediments of old sea floor and lakebeds. KARNA ORSEN
Below: Pillow basalt, ocean-floor magma that hardened quickly in seawater, retains its contorted form 50 million years later. ROBERT STEELQUIST
Facing page: Alternating layers of ash, mud, lava and debris revealed by erosion on Mt. Rainier tell of countless eruptions that gradually built the great stratovolcano. JEFF GNASS

theory-building have come in waves, adding pieces to the range of geologic thought. In Washington's mountains there are monuments to these theories; the literature of the Cascades, the Northern Rockies and the Olympics faithfully documents the construction of our state of knowledge.

Volcanism

Although the processes that shape our planet generally move slowly, passing unnoticed and playing out over time-spans beyond human memory, the explosive force by which magma leaves its subterranean kingdom rarely goes without attracting our attention—and has probably fostered in human society its own peculiar form of dread. Volcanoes give lie to the belief that the earth is patient. Local examples of past volcanic fury are common in the Washington mountainscape and recent events, especially the 1980 eruptions of Mt. St. Helens, have brought volcanism into the lives of most Pacific northwest residents.

Yet for all our experience with individual volcanoes, it is only recently that we have understood the earth as a volcanic system and seen the thread by which all volcanism is connected. That thread is most visible on the ocean floor, where a 48,000-mile volcanic crack encircles the globe. It is here that the youngest rock on the planet is found. Fresh oceanic crust that oozes out of the mid-ocean ridge cools quickly as it contacts seawater, taking a lumpy appearance. Because the lumps resemble pillows, this material is called "pillow basalt." The relationship between mountains and the oceanic ridge-vent system is readily visible—ancient volcanic seabed appears in many mountain formations.

Along the continental margins near this ridge volcanic activity is most intense. Because the Pacific ridge arcs along the coast of the Pacific northwest, Alaska and the Aleutian Islands and northeast Asia, the Pacific ocean rim is called the "Rim of Fire." Mountain ranges are found along this coastal belt and among them, volcanoes in various stages of quiescence. This active volcanic belt is a sign of constant churning action beneath us, of sea floor being forced into interior regions of the earth. Periodic episodes of volcanism have taken place in Washington over the last 200 million years, with long intervening passages of quiet.

The sequence of eruptions of Mt. St. Helens in 1980 made terms like "pyroclastic," and "dome-building" household buzzwords. Scientists and the general public alike received a home course in volcanism. One of the principal features of all northwest volcanoes that was particularly evident in the St. Helens eruptions is their extreme violence. This is partly due to the fact that magma is viscous, tending to clog its exit passageways rather than flow freely, as in the case of the oceanic volcanoes of Hawaii. Explosive forces within the magma chamber become partially choked, releasing their energy in fits. Cascades lava (mostly andesite and dacite) has a relatively high silica content and moves very slowly; because it is relatively cool, it doesn't move very far. Thus, it presents less of a direct threat than escaping gasses, flowing ash, debris and the mud that is created when rapidly melting glaciers lubricate and dislodge material on the mountain slopes.

The Cascade volcanoes each show us different aspects of volcanic action. Mt. Rainier, for example, reveals signs of a previous volcano much larger than the present mountain familiar to us. Geologists believe that Rainier once towered 16,000 feet above sea-level—about 1,500' higher than today. The surface rock we see has been badly eroded by glaciers and represents old lava and debris flows as well as some of the internal plumbing system of the volcano. Layers of ancient debris are visible in the crumbling ramparts of Little Tahoma, on Rainier's east flank, as well as in other exposures around the mountain.

Glacier Peak, hidden deep in the northern Cascades, has a very different history. The mountain grew slowly, quietly, filling the upper Suiattle River Valley and eventually growing over several adjacent ridges. After its gradual building process had proceeded for many thousands of years, Glacier Peak's temperament changed dramatically. In a violent explosion that occurred about 12,000 years ago, it spread ash throughout the Pacific northwest. Twelve miles downwind, a blanket of pumice covered the countryside to a depth of 12 feet. Although this relatively remote volcano has been quiet for several thousand years, new eruptions could announce its return to life—at any time.

Plate Tectonic Theory

No geologic theory has synthesized so much disparate evidence as the theory of plate tectonics. Seizing discarded elements of past explanations, like the continental drift idea espoused in 1915 by Alfred

The orderly pattern of columns visible in the Clear Fork Dacite Formation, near White Pass, reveals magma that shrank evenly as it slowly cooled. Facing page: Bonanza Peak, on the right, is Washington's highest non-volcanic peak (9,511'). Composed of gneiss, granite that has been partially remelted and hardened, Bonanza has resisted the erosive forces that have smoothed the unaltered granites of nearby Cloudy Peak. PAT O'HARA PHOTOS

Wegener and combining observations made with the use of complex ocean-floor mapping techniques, plate-tectonic theory created a foundation upon which most of contemporary earth science rests. It envisions a contra-dance in which a rind of continents and ocean floors floats on a sea of semi-fluid mantle called the asthenosphere. Since the beginning of time, these plate-like crustal rafts have moved over the surface of the earth sphere, combining and parting. Great supercontinents have formed and broken apart. One, known as Pangaea, is thought to have appeared 200 million years ago. Its subsequent break-up released vast chunks of plate material that drift and occasionally collide. Mountain ranges throughout the world appear to be linked to collisions and their results.

The significance of plate tectonic theory to Washington's ranges as a whole is that it describes a dynamism on the planet's surface. It posits powerful mechanisms by which uplift, horizontal movement and volcanic activity can be explained. The effects of localized structural phenomena, such as faulting and intrusion, make better sense when we can consider the plasticity of the whole region. And because implications of the theory are demonstrable over time, they illustrate principles that worked ages ago, at work now.

The Spreading Sea Floor

It would seem ironic that discussion of Washington's mountains should begin with a description of the sea-floor off our coast. It is here, however, that the forces that deform the surface of the planet are most evident. Research conducted in the 1960s and 1970s revealed intense volcanic activity along a ridge known as the East Pacific Rise, just off the Washington coast. Here, the Juan de Fuca plate is pushed eastward by deep heat currents within the mantle. Where the oceanic plates separate older deposits are forced away from the fissure at an even rate of between 3 and 8 centimeters per year. The ocean floor moves relentlessly toward the North American plate, carrying newly-formed basalt and sediments, which have accumulated on the ocean bottom, like a conveyer into a rock crusher.

As the sea floor approaches the continent, it is forced beneath the leading edge of the continental plate in a process known as subduction. Portions of the moving crust are carried to great depth beneath the continent's edge, where pressure and heat melt the rock. In liquid and gaseous form, the ocean basalts rise up through fissures and pipes within the continental mass. Where they surface, volcanic eruptions ensue. Where they remain trapped, they heat the surrounding material, often melting and combining with the continental rock to form large intrusions in the surrounding rock, called batholiths. Certain mountain ranges composed of granitic materials are actually batholiths that have had their overburden removed by forces of erosion.

Subducted material adds great thickness to the continental edge, often causing it to rise by flotation. Perhaps the best example of this is the Himalayas, where two

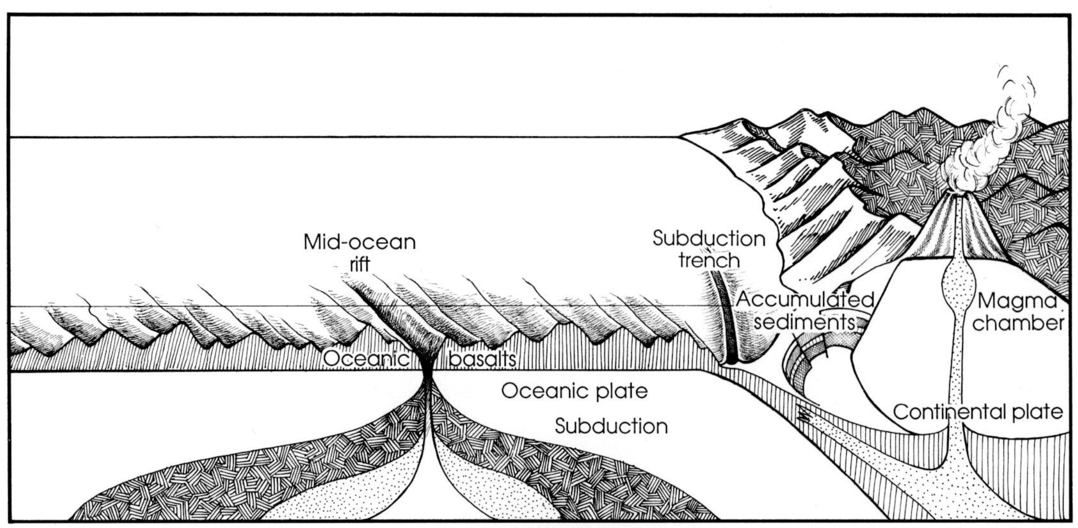

SUBDUCTION

Right: The "salt and pepper" appearance of granite, here from the Stuart Range, reveals the visible crystals that form when molten magma cools relatively slowly. The dark minerals are biotite and hornblende, the white crystals are feldspar and quartz.
PAT O'HARA

thicknesses of continental crust actually overlap. Where oceanic crust is subducted beneath other oceanic crust or a continental edge, the effect is not as dramatic, but contributes nonetheless to the uplift.

Not all of the spreading sea floor is drawn beneath the continent. Some is wedged between the converging plates and subjected to tremendous forces of lateral compression. Orderly layers of sediment become tangled arabesques. Once-horizontal bedding planes teeter skyward or dive into the earth; blocks buckle and fold and rotate, creating a confusing array of textures, colors and patterns, often with no apparent spatial relationship to their original positions. Whole regions can feel the pinch of converging plates and part of the process by which mountain regions rise is due to the fact that a given volume of material will bulge when it is squeezed too hard. Such squeezes are often relieved when large sheets separate and slide over one another in a process called "thrust faulting." Large portions of the North Cascades consist of material that has slid off its original footing and moved between six and 20 miles.

The Terrane Theory

The 1950s and 1960s were dramatic decades in geology. The general acceptance of plate tectonics theory revolutionized our interpretation of the dynamic earth. Certain more recent discoveries have prompted even more exciting news, however, and the development of a new generation of theory has special importance to our understanding of Washington mountain geology.

Scientists have long puzzled over the presence of discrete chunks of landscape in the midst of formations with which they share no apparent characteristics. One of the first of these areas to be studied and interpreted is known as Wrangellia, because the bulk of the formation is located in the Wrangell Mountains of southeastern Alaska. Wrangellia posed significant problems because it bears no resemblance to its surroundings. To the surprise of geologists, magnetic properties within the rocks indicate that the rock was formed somewhere within close proximity to the equator. In a bold extension of plate tectonic theory, geologists have concluded that certain small masses of crust actually move faster and farther than was previously thought possible, and have been smeared along the edges of continental plates. Such bodies are known as "suspect terranes," or simply, "terranes."

Sedimentary rocks formed in regular layers tilt crazily here on Mt. Angeles, as a result of pressures and upheaval caused by shifting continental plates. ROSS HAMILTON

Portions of Wrangellia appear to comprise not only southeastern Alaska, but the Queen Charlotte Islands, Vancouver Island and perhaps even some of the region dissected by Hells Canyon in eastern Oregon and western Idaho. The discontinuous and elongated pattern suggested by the occurrence of Wrangellia implies that it broke up as it contacted the continental plate—that parts of it rubbed off during a prolonged collision and remain where they became embedded in the continental edge. Although Wrangellia itself does not contribute to our understanding of Washington's ranges, other terranes are thought to have played an important part in the assembly of what is now Washington.

According to David Alt and Donald Hyndman, in their book *Roadside Geology of Washington,* the plastering of several suspect terranes onto the growing margin of the continent was part of the succession of structural events that built our mountain ranges. They speculate that in the last 200 million years, two large island masses collided with the advancing western edge of North America. During each of these "docking" events, a subduction zone was formed as the terranes drew near the continent, which generated volcanic activity inland on the continent. Each subduction trench was overridden just prior to the collision and the debris that was bulldozed into the trench was forcefully added to the continental front. As each terrane contacted the continental plate, it underwent massive deformation, resulting in a mountain-building episode. In this scenario, the Okanogan Highlands and the oldest Cascade Range each represent distinct terranes—island fragments caught on conveyor belts of old sea floor that was on a collision course with North America.

Movements such as these would not seem possible if they didn't occasionally burst upon us in the form of eruptions or earthquakes. We see the lines in the rock, the folds, the looping forms. We see the cooked rock, blue and compressed. It somehow doesn't register until, seized by fright or merely curious, we hear the volcano peal or feel the ground shudder. The earth is moving. Even without this experience we may find signs when we see cycles and understand that returnings are a rule on a planet rolling in space. There is just so much material on earth and it has just so many places to go. Like the sun, dropping now beyond the range, it will come up again once it has gone under.

Facing page: Fine-grained sandstone, upthrust to form Blue Mountain along the northern edge of the Olympics, was formed as tiny particles collected on the floor of the ocean eons ago that were slowly compressed into a consolidated mass.

Left: Eldorado Peak (8,868'), massive and glacier-cloaked, straddles the Cascade Crest in one of the most dramatic alpine regions of Washington State. It is composed of highly metamorphosed rock that characterizes the "crystalline core" of the range.

PAT O'HARA PHOTOS

CHAPTER TWO

MOUNTAIN CARVING

Along Spirit Lake trail. TOM & PAT LEESON

The combined forces of gravity, chemical weathering, glacial erosion and surface water runoff dissect mountain faces into a multitude of broken surfaces. Mt. Stuart (9,415') is a massive block of granite that reveals erosion in its many forms. PAT O'HARA

It was the 19th century American geologist Clarence E. Dutton who said that erosion is to geology what gravity is to astronomy. In the great budget of earthly substance, material carried by the agents of erosion—gravity, water, wind and ice—is redistributed and reordered, laid in distinctive patterns and given a new beginning. Eventually, it will be deformed and lifted, or sucked into the maw of colliding plates where it will roast, and emerge physically and chemically transformed. Dutton also elaborated the concept of isostasy, the process by which the earth's sphere attends to its roundness. Isostasy postulates that continents float, that their roots extend berglike into the mantle about five to ten times the distance that their peaks protrude into the sky. Taken together, the laws of erosion and isostasy imply the surface of the planet as a slowly rebounding membrane, of high places always flowing to low, of renewal and redistribution of the mass of the earth's surface.

We, therefore, should not be surprised to find that mountains, in addition to being the seat of upheaval, are the earth's principal areas of erosion. The Himalaya Range, by itself, contributes about 40 percent of all of material being eroded on earth at any given time. Put simply, what goes up must come down.

In Washington, the signs of erosion in the mountains are found throughout the landscape. Spits and bars along our coasts consist of fine materials which, at one time or another, were part of the mountains. Boulders that litter the Puget Lowland arrived as the overburden of Pleistocene glaciers. Ash mixed into the wind-laid soils of the Columbia Plateau was exhaled in hot mountain breaths. Rivers that writhe milky in flood carry the gouged shoulders of mountain horns and aretes, piece by microscopic piece. Whole cities and suburbs lie perched on mudflows that swallowed valley bottoms. Even the submarine canyons in the continental shelf form channels through which surge the stuff of former mountains, en route to the ultimate low ground—the abyss.

And although much can be said of the youth of Washington's mountains in terms of their uplift and formation, it is their eroded surfaces that give them their fresh appearance. Erosion sharpens the relief by sweeping away enclosing debris, honing ridges into blades, advancing into the core of mountain blocks, exposing the hardest minerals and stripping away the soft. It is water that has had the greatest shaping touch on Washington's mountainous face. In its gaseous state, water effects

Troublesome Creek, originating in the North Cascades' Columbia Glacier, foams through its narrow course. Polished rock attests to the grinding action of the stream's sediment load.
PAT O'HARA

only minor changes in rock, weathering it slightly. But its sibling forms, liquid and solid, pluck and deliver whole ranges, piece by piece, to the ocean floor.

Weathering

The most fundamental of all the processes of erosion is that by which rock weakens. Weathering occurs with great subtlety, breaking chemical bonds, separating grain from grain, pitting the smooth, fracturing the solid—all advancing the effects of gasses of the atmosphere, chemicals in rainwater, soil runoff, the root hairs of plants and the physical forces of expansion and contraction imposed by temperature. Weathering is the aging process of rock surfaces. It is the process that must precede the other, more active, forms of erosion.

In many forms of mountain rock, inherent weaknesses hasten weathering. Ocean-bottom basalt, for instance, shatters as it cools in seawater, rendering it relatively porous from the outset. Basalt deposits often reveal quartz veins where, deep in the bowels of a mountain range, water has percolated through the basalt formation, leaving silica deposits like so much scale in old plumbing. Once hoisted onto the shoulders of the land, basalt weathers quickly, even though it is a fairly hard and dense substance.

Sedimentary rocks—sandstones and shales—are laid down as distinct layers, with distinct bedding planes. As a result, they fracture very easily along those planes, admitting water into the cleavages. Limestone, another sedimentary rock, reacts chemically to the presence of acids, which occur naturally in plant roots, groundwater and rain. Exposure to these agents gradually deteriorates limestone, leaving it weakened and vulnerable to other forces.

Even the crystalline structure of rock affects its rate of weathering. Feldspar fragments embedded in granite expand slightly in reaction to certain chemicals, weakening their bonds with the matrix around them. In other rock, crystals that nest tightly are more weather-resistant than those with irregular adjoining surfaces.

Weathering is a very real concern to the rockclimber, for it is the force that renders brittle rock "rotten," and easily loosened. Combined with gravity, its own passive transport system, weathering attacks the surface of the mountains, softening, fissuring the material and sluffing away grains and pebbles. It opens the footholds for frost and runoff—initiating the slow leveling of the ranges.

Facing page: The Southern Pickets viewed from the north. Ice crystals trail from the summits as an arctic high-pressure system cleanses the air. Principal summits on the background ridge are, from left, McMillan Spire, Inspiration Peak, Mt. Degenhardt (with Degenhardt Glacier), Mt. Terror and Twin Needles. Luna Peak is in the foreground. PAT O'HARA

Above: Weathering, the chemical process by which minerals dissolve and rock grains separate, is hastened by mild acids given off by plants. Kettle Range granite shows the softening signs of interaction with living organisms. ROBERT STEELQUIST

Moving Water

Water as a liquid is a light, flexible, and extraordinarily mobile substance. It infiltrates the tiniest pores, falling to gravity or wicking upward or sideways because of its capillary attraction to itself. As a fluid medium, it also carries many other substances. A raindrop, for example, will enclose and carry dust particles and the molecules of other substances. As groundwater, chemical and mineral leachates will flow through bedrock fissures, shuffled along by water. As a rivulet, water will carry silt grains and roll pebbles. As a raging flood, it will dislodge boulders,

At its snout (above), the Carbon Glacier ends and the Carbon River begins—boiling cloudy with minute particles of Mt. Rainier.
Lake Crescent, on the northern edge of the Olympic Mountains, occupies a typically broad, U-shaped valley carved by continental glaciers that visited the Puget Lowland region as recently as 12,000 years ago.
PAT O'HARA PHOTOS

dribbling them along a quick, murky streambed like basketballs running amok. Water dissolves. It dilutes and lubricates. Water running over tilted land accelerates quickly, and as its velocity increases, so does its transporting ability and the battering-ram destructiveness of its cargo.

Water undercuts steep slopes, removing the foundations of mountain walls. More debris falls, waiting in line to be carried away itself. Debris heaps lodge in momentary repose at steep angles; water efficiently conducts them away.

Water characteristically carves V-shaped valleys. This is because, unlike glaciers, rivers and streams leave the land quickly and cannot absorb and carry all of the loose material in a valley at the same time. The only active site of water erosion is in the streambed itself, a relatively narrow area. Gravity delivers the rock to the water; gravity and water do the rest.

Glaciation

We are not quite sure what events trigger the onset of an Ice Age. Some theorists have suggested that ash clouds belched into the atmosphere during periods of intense volcanic activity screen the earth from warmth, starting a global cooling. In such a cooling, the summer period of melting is shortened and the winter period of freezing is lengthened. A long series of cool summers enables the accumulated snow to sit, and as it sits, undergo physical changes in its crystalline structure that transform it to glacial ice. As its overburden increases with subsequent layers of snow, glacier ice compresses. With enough pressure it becomes a plastic substance, deforming and flowing. Its movement, internally and over its rock bed, makes it a sluggish river capable of transporting great quantities of rock debris. As it flows, fragments entrapped in the glacier sole gnaw at the pavement, leaving distinctive striations in the bed. A thin sheet of water, ice melted by the pressure of the overlying ice, flushes away the finest debris. Glacier-born rivers run cloudy with the flour ground in the ice-mill.

The Anatomy of a Glacier

A living glacier is a tilted moonscape of white. Bizarre forms cover its surface; blocks, lumps, cuplike ripples. Yawning crevasses score the surface, issuing a weird blue from within. Early in the season, the glacier exudes the ambience of a vast, docile snowdrift, and scrambling over it is a direct affair: gaze upon a distant point and plod heavily until you reach it. But route-finding in late summer resembles running a maze. Frustration and dread run neck and neck as impasses and architecturally suspect snowbridges reveal themselves. Each step forward is matched, measure for measure, with caution. You dance lightly, as if the ice were thin.

A glacier is more than an ice-filled basin or valley. It is a finely tuned system, a budget, with a tender balance between growing and shrinking. In general, two zones are found on a glacier. They reflect the credit and debit columns of the glacier's budget. The credit side is the accumulation zone. This is the area of the glacier where newly fallen snow rests, and remains through the summer season so that it can be added to the glacier's bulk. On the

Above: Moisture-laden maritime air currents feed the active glacier system of Mt. Olympus—which reaches farther into the lowland than any other in the world at its latitude. PAT O'HARA

Left: Streaked with debris it has entombed for decades, the Humes Glacier snout on Mt. Olympus bears precariously on polished boulders. © GARY BRAASCH

ANATOMY OF A GLACIER

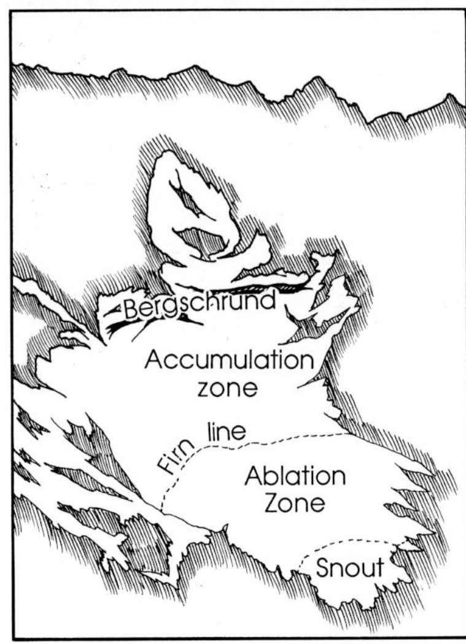

Near right: The freeze-thaw cycle exploits natural fractures in rock. In glaciers, the ice actually "plucks" fissured blocks out of surrounding material. PAT O'HARA *Far right: Where glacier ice's plasticity is insufficient to adjust to stresses of its flow, the ice cracks, forming crevasses.* PAT O'HARA *Facing page: Mt. Baker's north face reveals the erosive power of Roosevelt and Coleman glaciers.* PAT O'HARA PHOTOS

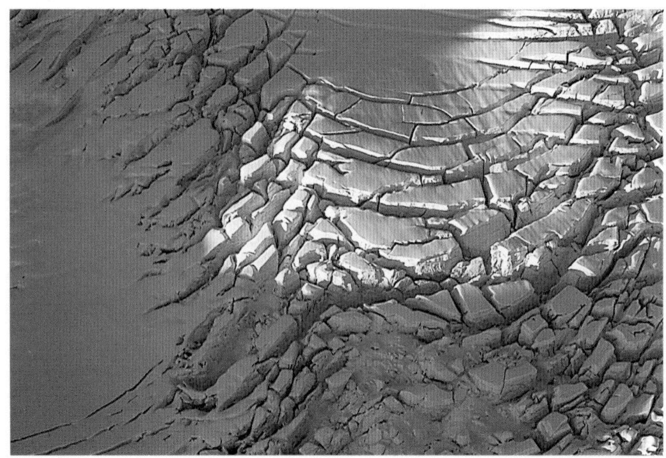

debit side is the ablation zone. This is the area of the glacier where more ice melts than gathers. When accumulation exceeds ablation, a glacier grows. When ablation exceeds accumulation, the glacier shrinks.

Ablation and accumulation zones are readily apparent on a glacier. The ablation zone usually is found nearest the glacier's snout. During late summer, when the melt cycle is at its peak, the ablation zone will have advanced up the glacier. The ablation zone will consist of streaked and dirty raw ice—signs that the glacier's uppermost layers are melting.

The accumulation zone wears its mantle of snow from the previous winter. This snow, not yet incorporated into the glacial body, has not undergone the metamorphosis into glacier ice. Scientists refer to it as firn; its boundary with the ablation zone is called the firn line. The movement of the firn line up the glacier with the progression of summer indicates the condition of the glacier's budget. A rapid journey up the glacier represents a net loss for the year. A slow journey partway up probably represents a gain.

A glacier that moves over uneven terrain is subject to many internal stresses and strains. And while the ice is relatively plastic, flowing around objects and surfaces, it frequently moves too quickly to relieve the stress with its plasticity. It breaks. It cracks and fractures and forms into blocks that shuffle and fall. The cracks are called crevasses. Where the glacier tumbles over a lip in its basin it forms an icefall. Crevasse patterns reveal the topography of the glacier bed and the movement of the flowing ice. A downward bend creates crevasses that run across the glacier. If steep enough an icefall ensues. Where a glacier meets an upward bend, surface crevasses close. As a glacier rounds a bend, crevasses open along the outer edge of the bend. When a glacier surges forward, broad curving crevasses bulge toward the snout.

Where the upper end of a moving glacier tears itself from its mountain host a large crevasse forms, known as a bergschrund. The jumble of blocks that forms the

glacier's snout is a constantly changing icefall—the daily discharge of tumbling blocks booms through the mountains, like the sounds of monster boxcars being bumped in a freight yard.

The Glacial Landscape

Washingtonians don't have to look far for evidence of past glaciation. The bluffs that line Puget Sound consist of glacier-laid gravels. The whole Puget Trough was blanketed by an ice sheet as recently as 12,000 years ago. Much of eastern Washington was scoured by the flood released when a vast lake spilled through the Columbia Basin following the rotting of its glacier-dam. By far the greatest evidence is in the areas where glacial remnants continue to rasp at mountain masses. Most of Washington's glaciers have retreated into the strongholds of their cirque basins. Many are indistinguishable from perennial snowfields. The largest, occupying the broad flanks of major peaks like Mt. Rainier, Mt. Baker, Mt. Olympus, and Mt. Adams, seem to wrap their respective peaks like capes. During summer months they radiate away from the summits, dirty with debris that has fallen from surrounding rock walls.

Active glacial landscapes reveal much of the age of glacial processes. A glacier begins forming in a high valley, where increasing amounts of snow accumulate. Gradually, glacier ice forms. Just as it inches downhill, spilling into lower country as it grows, it chews away at the headwall and sidewalls of its basin, forming a glacial cirque, often shaped like a bucket seat. The steepness of the cirque walls is maintained as the ice literally plucks blocks and boulders out of the walls, through the process of freeze and thaw, and then transports them away, trapped in ice.

Glacial erosion gradually causes a cirque to deepen as erosion carves backward into the mountain. As glaciers work on opposite sides of a ridge, cirques deepen toward each other, leaving only a thin sawtoothed ridge between them. Peaks with several active glaciers working around them slowly steepen into horns—jagged three- or four-sided spires.

Glacial landscapes consist not only of the zones of erosion where rock is being or has been removed, but also of the areas where the material has been laid. These consist of debris heaps called moraines—piles left by the bulldozing action of glaciers. Terminal moraines represent the farthest extent of glaciation—crescent-shaped mounds that once wrapped around the glacier's snout. Lateral moraines outline the glacier's flanks. Often a sequence of glacial advances and retreats can be seen as the faint outlines of revegetated moraines.

Country once inhabited by glaciers displays other telltale signs of icy visitations. Erratics—boulders that originated far away—are deposited where the shrinking glacier dropped them. Glistening slabs of bedrock can show the striations worn by the filing action of rock fragments embedded in the glacier's sole. Clay deposits with their telltale colonies of horsetails often betray an ancient lake-bottom, where a glacier dammed a river valley. And hardpan, the bane of home gardeners, often has another name—glacial till. It consists of glacier deposits pressed into a dense cake by the weight of glacial ice.

A deglaciated landscape is a clean landscape, spare in its signs of living things. Crystal-clear lakes, devoid of all but the most pioneering of life-forms, dot the recently uncovered basins of the high country. Soil must be formed before the land can nourish life. Lichens begin the reclamation, followed by the entire sequence of succession. In time, forests intrude. Slowly, the process of erratic dismemberment of the land gives way to the reordering imposed by living things.

It is clear that for all their bulk and magnificence the mountains of Washington are gradually being reduced by the forces of erosion. The time scale in which this occurs is incomprehensible. Even the Ice Age, 10,000 years distant, is known to us only because we leave our senses momentarily and reason ourselves backward, squinting at the landscape to blur its present. Processes are at work, however, that change the mountains. The taste of cloudy glacier runoff in a metal cup, the distant rumbles of a hanging glacier intruding on our restless sleep, the echo of a rockfall descending a dry gully—all of these speak to relentless change.

If it is any consolation, the roots of our present mountains descend into the roots of other, older ranges. The denudation that we glimpse in tiny, scattered events, has overcome Washington ranges that stood prior to these. The avalanches of a thousand years ago continue to spread down the slopes of the continental shelf. On the ocean floor old mountains rest, spread into sheets and ready for another orogenic assembly. Today's Cascades, Olympics, Rockies are the benefactors of the mountains that will emerge in a distant tomorrow.

Facing page: Encrusting lichens and penstemon represent the vanguard of recolonizers of a laterial moraine of retreating Anderson Glacier in the Olympics. PAT O'HARA *Above: Forming a landscape of sharp contrast, Mt. Baker's Coleman Glacier cuts deeply into Chowder Ridge.* PAT O'HARA *Far left: Glacial striae, the scratch marks left by rock particles embedded in the sole of a glacier reveal the abrasive power of moving ice.* KARNA ORSEN *Left: Vivid splashes of lichens are among the first signs of the awakening life in a deglaciated landscape.* PAT O'HARA

THE LITTLE ICE AGE

Glacial systems represent a finely-tuned balance of temperature, precipitation and cloud cover. Just as the fossil record reveals details of life-forms and conditions of the distant past, the glacial record preserves climatic features of past eras. Global cycles of cooling and warming have triggered advances and retreats of the earth's glaciers. Sequences of these events are revealed in glacial landscapes. Vast portions of the continents show signs of major Ice Ages, signals that the global climate has had great swings from warm to cold, and then back to warm. In the most specific sense, day-to-day temperature fluctuations affect the way glaciers behave, causing slight flow surges and daily periods of icefall activity.

Cycles of intermediate duration consist of periods lasting several centuries. One such event, faithfully recorded in the glacial landscape of Washington's ranges is the Little Ice Age, approximately four centuries of cooling that affected most of the northern hemisphere. Fortunately, the glacial record is corroborated by historical accounts of other signs of the cool-weather trend that apparently began about 1500 A.D. and lasted until about 1920.

The best evidence in Washington of the Little Ice Age is found in the relative movement of glacier snouts and the rock heaps that accumulate there. Terminal moraines are the fingerprints that reveal the extent of past advances. A variety of methods, including the study of lichens that pioneer freshly deglaciated rockfields, the analysis of pollen, tree-ring analysis, observing signs of past timberlines and the use of carbon dating, have enabled scientists to piece together details of the climate during this not-too-distant past. In addition, photographs, journal accounts and agricultural records correlate strongly with the glacial record.

Studies conducted on Dome Peak and in the North Cascades, the Nisqually Glacier of Mt. Rainier and the Blue Glacier of Mt. Olympus, have revealed local effects of a period when the globe cooled—famine gripped Iceland, sea-ice visited Scotland, Washington's troops shivered at Valley Forge, and timberline retreated downward through many of the northwest's mountain ranges. In spite of slightly differing schedules of retreat and advance due to local differences in climatic conditions, all show the faint imprint of the Little Ice Age.

Dome Peak is a broad, glacier-covered massif in the north-central Cascades. Several of its glaciers have been studied in an attempt to reconstruct their behavior during the Little Ice Age. One, the South Cascade Glacier, appears to have been most extensive sometime during the 16th and 17th centuries. It retreated only slightly through the 19th century and then very abruptly in the early 20th century. Altogether, its retreat has covered 4,460 feet.

Shrinkage of the Nisqually Glacier, on Mt. Rainier's south flank, has been observed since the mountain was first explored in 1857 by Lt. August V. Kautz. Since then, the terminus has been receding except for brief advances, which occurred in short periods between 1905 and 1908, 1964 and 1969, and 1975 and 1979. According to a U.S Geological Survey report released in 1984, the Nisqually Glacier has retreated 6,379 feet and advanced 964 feet since Kautz's observation in 1857.

The importance of Little Ice Age studies lie in their revelation of the delicate tuning of alpine glacier systems to trends of cooling and heating that affect the global weather system. Localized phenomena vary the sensitivity of any given glacier, yet these glaciers provide us with dramatic evidence of climatic history. And, if the past reveals any glimpses of the future, climatic events triggered by what some scientists call the "greenhouse effect," the warming of the earth's atmosphere because of the buildup of carbon dioxide, would affect our alpine glacier systems. Such a global warmup would profoundly affect our mountainous terrain and its zonal distribution of plant and animal communities.

Facing page: Approximately 50 years separate these historic views of the Blue Glacier snout on Mt. Olympus. The upper photograph was taken in 1912—approximately the end of the Little Ice Age—and shows the Blue Glacier icefall tumbling deep into the canyon of Glacier Creek, a tributary of the Hoh River. By 1962, when the lower photograph was taken, the glacier had retreated significantly; its icefall barely reached the canyon brink. COURTESY OLYMPIC NATIONAL PARK, PORT ANGELES.

Above: Mt. Rainier's Nisqually Glacier has been in nearly constant retreat since approximately 1840, when it reached its Little Ice Age maximum. Although short advances have temporarily checked the shrinkage, the Nisqually is now more than one mile shorter than in 1857, when its terminus position was first observed. PAT O'HARA

CHAPTER THREE

LIFE OF MOUNTAINS

Pika. TOM & PAT LEESON

Succulent stems and leaves and the rosette form of stonecrop are adaptations to dryness—just one of the factors that mountain plants must overcome to survive. PAT O'HARA

The province of ice and rock is a strangely quiet place. The signs of life diminish with elevation. First it is the forest that falls away, gradually, as finger-like patches intrude upward into meadow. Trees decrease in size; many take the appearance of religiously clipped shrubs. Deciduous plants like mountain ash, huckleberry, blueberry and heather have lithe stems that bend to the ground under the load of winter snow. Sedges and heather mat the bare ground in patches—sedges in depressions where moisture and fine soil accumulate, heather in better-drained soil mixed with the organic matter of its own decaying roots and leaves. Gradually, only dwarfed cushions of foliage are seen, on wind-swept ridges and in the scant shelter afforded between rocks. Showy blossoms bloom briefly, blatant advertisements for scarce pollinators. Flowers also vanish as we climb, replaced by boulder-encrusting lichen, in hues that span the range from vivid to dull. This is not a hospitable place. It is a place where even the tracks of animals reveal few pauses in transit. Mountain goats and bear traverse the divide to find better sustenance on its opposite slope.

Yet for their apparent lifelessness, mountain ranges have forged the patterns of life over whole continents and contributed greatly to the survival and evolution of species over time.

Mountains sustain an incredible variety of plants and wildlife, often because their rugged terrain has not felt the taming of civilization. Mountain strongholds contain lingering populations of predators that long ago disappeared from domesticated range and low country. In Washington, grizzly bear, timber wolf, moose and mountain caribou hang on to a tendril of existence because territory we humans covet remains beyond our grasp; the mountain keep is theirs. Patterns of plant distribution remain relatively unaltered in mountain ranges because we have not replaced the natural patchwork of plant types with the few species that we cultivate for timber, food and livestock and the weedy tag-alongs that benefit from our disturbances.

Mountains interject variety into climate and topography, harboring organisms that are specialists at living under the harshest of conditions. Mountain ranges, like oceans, form barriers that preclude colonization of discontinuous lowland by cosmopolitan interlopers. They restrict the interchange of genetic information, concentrating in local populations the traits that best assure survival. Boundaries in many senses, mountains divide continents into regions that contain their own distinct associations of living things.

Washington's mountains are critical relict fragments of the once boundless North American wilderness. The only remaining wolves, caribou, grizzly bears and wolverines in the state rely on isolated pockets of mountainous terrain in the extreme north and east of Washington for survival. JESS R. LEE

Mountain ranges also create distinct layers in vertical space, where living things sort themselves according to tolerances for environmental conditions and where competition is keen. In its coarse form, this pattern is reflected in timberlines. On a more subtle level, such layering manifests itself in the upper and lower elevation limits for many species of plants and animals.

In a theory advanced by American zoologist Clinton Hart Merriam (1855-1942), animals and plants thrive only within a certain elevation range, where temperature and other factors influence the organisms' ability to survive. Merriam's principle became known as the Life-Zone concept and, although it fails to describe all of the complexities of plant and animal distribution, it provides a functional model for interpreting how elevation affects living things.

Top: Many natural factors impose the vegetation boundary of timberline (Olympic N.P.). Right: Low-bush huckleberries in autumn, before snowdrifts insulate them (Olympic N.P.). Above: Twisted trunks and wood abraded by windborne ice attest to harsh conditions in subalpine regions, as here near La Bohn Gap, Alpine Lakes Wilderness. PAT O'HARA PHOTOS

Merriam observed distinct color layers in Arizona's San Francisco Peaks—bands of different shades of vegetation, representing strata of plant communities dominated by particular groups of species. To each of these bands he assigned a name chosen because of the similarity between that zone and a major region of latitude. Hence the highest elevation zone was called the Arctic Zone. The next highest the Hudsonian (for Hudson's Bay), followed by the Canadian, the Humid Transition, the Arid Transition, and the Sonoran. Merriam's terminology has largely been replaced by naming the appropriate zone after the dominant plant or physiographic name for the area (subalpine, montane, lowland, etc.)

Using the Life-Zone concept, we can not only identify particular features of the array of living things in a single mountain range, but also compare the effects of elevation on organisms of different ranges. We can, for instance, observe that as we move away from the coast, zones move up—the subalpine zone in the Olympics (marked by upper timberline) can be found as low as 4,000 feet above sea-level; in the Cascades, it ranges between 5,000 and 8,000 feet. In the Rockies, the subalpine zone can start between 7,500 and 9,500 feet. A similar effect occurs from north to south. Timberline in Denali National Park in Alaska occurs at approximately 2,000 feet—in Colorado's Rocky Mountain National Park, at approximately 10,000 to 11,000 feet. This basis for comparison provides a valuable tool for understanding the environmental mechanisms that dictate plant and animal distribution. It is a unifying theme that plays with minor variation throughout Washington's mountains.

By far the most conspicuous living boundary imposed on an upthrust piece of land is its timberline. Timberline evokes the weathered look of stunted copses, pruned into aerodynamic forms, or straight cone-shaped trees, living replicas of Old-World church steeples, designed, it would seem, to shed snow. Timberline, sometimes visible as a distinct line on a distant slope, is really a broad band in which forest and meadow interfinger and where isolated clusters of trees progressively get smaller until trees vanish altogether.

This upper limit is affected by several factors which work together to form a complex set of conditions for life. Exposure to wind means that trees are severely punished by the sandblast effects of airborne ice crystals. Silver wood, scalped of its bark and bleached by harsh sunlight testifies to the extremes. Strong winds also may carry away accumulated snow, depriving the tree of the reservoir of moisture needed during the summer period of drought.

The overabundance of snow, in localized patches, can prevent tree seedlings from taking hold. Lingering snow patches delay the arrival of spring, compressing the short season in which seedlings must sprout, grow and harden into a few weeks—insufficient time for the tree to grow strong enough to withstand the killing frosts of the early alpine autumn.

Slope aspect—the compass direction that a slope faces—also plays an important role in determining the elevation at which trees cease to be the dominant life-forms. Typically, shady north-facing slopes support forests at a higher elevation than the parched south side. Exceptions to this rule include north slopes only recently unburdened of their alpine glaciers. In such places, timberline may be dictated by the presence of late-lying snowfields or the availability of soil, the product of post-glacial succession in which forests are latecomers.

In Washington, mountains form boundaries of the major climatic zones of the state. Since climatic conditions also shape the communities of living things, east- and west-side vegetation contrast sharply. Our mountain ranges occupy belts that run parallel to the coast, thus figuring prominently in the precipitation variations between the maritime and interior regions.

The ocean is a great moderator of climates, a stable heat-sink that rarely changes more than a few degrees in temperature. Water that has evaporated from the Pacific flows landward in cloud masses and surging storm systems. As it reaches the coast it rises, forced over the abruptly rising topography. Cooling as it gains elevation, it condenses, falling as rain or snow. The western slope of the Olympics receives the brunt of this precipitation, with 150 inches of rain falling every year in places like the Hoh and Quinault Valleys. The western Olympic summits receive a like amount in the form of snow—greatly expanded in volume. Hence, the glaciers of Olympus can accumulate more than 100 feet of snow in a year.

Downstream of the mountains precipitation already has been wrung from the clouds and a condition called "rain shadow" prevails. Northeast of the Olympics, precipitation rarely exceeds 18 inches per year. Thus, the Olympics form a barrier between the wettest and the driest areas of western Washington. Vegetation differences are dramatic. Sitka spruce dominates the rain-forest valleys

Moist, mid-elevation forests cloak the western mountain slopes. PAT O'HARA

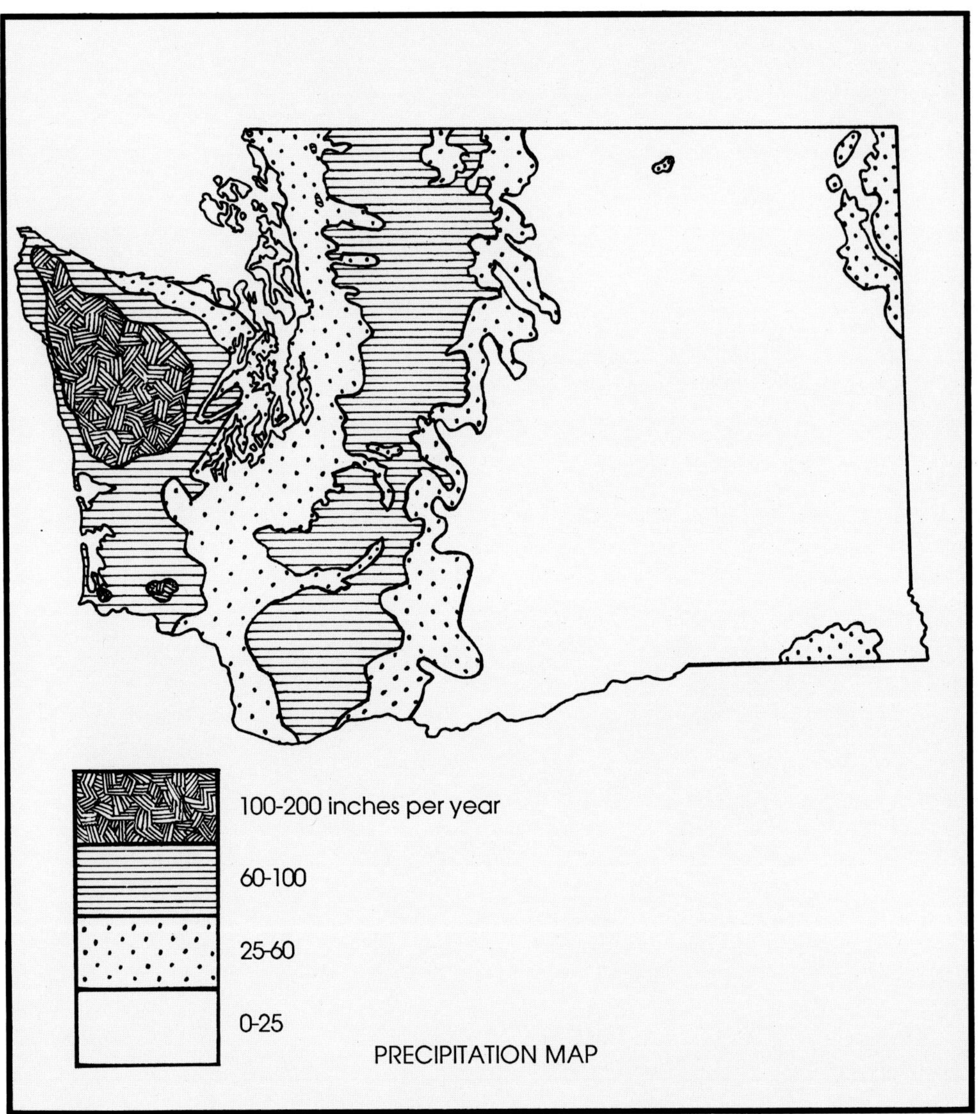

of the wet west side; oak and cactus share the gravel moraines bordering the dry prairie of the Dungeness Valley and the rocky shores of the San Juan Islands.

The rain-shadow effect of the Olympics is repeated on a grander scale in the lee of the Cascades. Towering almost twice the height of Olympus, Mt. Rainier collects a mantle of snow often 200 feet deep over the course of a year. Rainfall in the western lowlands of Mt. Rainier National Park creates temperate rain-forest conditions similar to those of the Olympic coastal valleys. East of the Cascades, the parched Columbia plateau receives less than 15 inches of annual precipitation. The mountain boundary dramatically influences the climate, itself the keystone of conditions with which every living thing must contend.

Parent country is the term geologists use to characterize the materials that comprise a mountain massif. Parent country is the stuff of which soils are made from the weathered crumbs of mountains. Soil exerts its own set of conditions on plant forms and soils containing particular minerals often host special populations and communities of plants. Soils derived from serpentine parent country contain high concentrations of magnesium, nickel and chromium, but are lacking in calcium, nitrogen and phosphorus. Serpentine outcrops in the Wenatchee Mountains are home to several plants not found elsewhere. These include the Wenatchee Mountain lomatium, a distant relative of the carrot. The Shasta fern is found in numerous mountain ranges in the western hemisphere including the Wenatchee Mountains—only if serpentine soils are present.

Climatic and chemical regimes are two good examples of the role that mountain ranges play in determining the distribution of plants. But mountains also affect the distribution of animals in very profound ways. For animals that have honed their adaptive advantage over the millenia to be suited to mountain environments and not lowlands, mountains are critical refuges of discrete gene pools. Consider, for example, the marmot. Marmots are found throughout the world's mountain ranges. Large members of the squirrel family, and closely related to woodchucks, marmots inhabit the high meadows and rockfields of western North America, nourished by succulent meadow plants like lupine, grasses and sedges. Long mountain winters blow over them, unnoticed as marmots hibernate deep in their burrows. Elaborate social behavior characterizes marmot life. Large groups of marmots often live as colonies where there is adequate space, food and soil for burrows. In Washington, four species of marmot inhabit our mountain and high plateau regions—spatially divided into units that correspond with geographic and elevation boundaries imposed by mountains. Washington's marmots are the eastern woodchuck, the hoary marmot, the yellow-bellied marmot and the Olympic marmot.

The eastern woodchuck is limited to middle elevations of mountainous regions that connect to Rocky Mountain ranges of British Columbia. The hoary marmot is found high in the subalpine regions of the Cascades and Rockies. The frost-grey pelage of this animal makes it particularly well suited to live in areas composed of granitic rock—some authorities believe that this camouflage advantage has affected the marmot's distribution. The yellow-bellied marmot is a meadow marmot found at lower elevations in the Cascades, adjacent to open prairie land and in mountainous regions where the hoary marmot is absent. This could suggest that where the two species must compete, the hoary has an advantage; where they do not compete, its brownish cousin can hold its own.

The Olympic marmot is found only in the subalpine regions of the Olympic Mountains, separated from its continental relatives by the intervening lowland and salt water of the Puget Sound region. Slight variations in color and skull proportions indicate that this animal has advanced along its own pathway of survival, perhaps for several million years.

Distribution of the marmots in Washington reveals the importance of isolation mechanisms afforded by several factors inherent in mountain ranges. Variety of elevation, continuity of ranges as migration routes, discontinuity of ranges as migration routes and even the adaptive value of coloration suited to specific parent country reveal a glove-like fit between organism and environment. In each case, narrow habitat requirements based on the suitability of specific environments to each species have served to isolate the respective gene pools. Mountains, in their vertical and horizontal spatial arrangements, have maintained boundaries necessary for the distinct species to evolve separately and remain separate.

Although a wide variety of animals can survive only in mountain ranges, gaps in ranges can mean that animals common to one range may not exist in another where

Mountains, or their absence, impose geographic barriers to the flow of genes from one population of organisms to another. Washington's marmots are spatially separated into units neatly occupied by different species. Washington marmots include (clock-wise from upper left): the yellow-bellied marmot, an inhabitant of lower Cascades meadows and adjacent prairies TIM CHRISTIE; *the Olympic marmot, separated from the other marmots by the Puget lowland* MIKE LOGAN; *and the hoary marmot, distributed throughout the Cascades subalpine, particularly in areas with exposed granite.* TOM & PAT LEESON

Above: Black tail deer and her fawn after early summer snowfall. TOM & PAT LEESON

Right: The lynx is generally absent from areas west of the Cascades but small numbers roam the remote mountainous areas in the north-eastern part of the state. TOM ULRICH

Facing page: The blaze of alpine larch against the season's first snow hints of winter's arrival. In the mountain world the lengthening shadows of autumn remind us that the hold of life is precarious in a landscape so filled with extremes. PAT O'HARA

one would expect to find them because it is isolated by a moat of lowland. Bighorn sheep, lynx, porcupine, red fox, wolverine, pika and mountain goat apparently never inhabited the Olympics although their presence in nearby ranges suggests that suitable habitat always has existed on the Olympic Peninsula. Red fox and mountain goats did colonize the Olympic Peninsula, but only with the help of modern man. Among other things, the "missing seven" reinforce the notion that the Olympic Range has been, for its 50 million years of existence, a mountain mass distinct from its surrounding ranges.

Another role that mountains play over the eons in the shaping of life-forms is that of refuge during Ice Age inundations. Alpine glacier systems are known to respond to climatic variations at different rates than continental glacier systems. As a result, the smaller systems which originate in the mountain ranges advance and retreat many times in the same period of time it takes a continental system to advance and retreat just once. Using this logic, scientists reason that ice-free areas within the Washington mountain ranges have existed at the same times that lowland areas were choked with ice. These refugia, as they are called, provide some startling explanations for plants and animals that, by all rights, should have become extinct when Pleistocene glaciers overran much of Washington state.

Mountain range refugia can be viewed as islands when you consider that separation by expanses of lowland can be just as effective as separation by expanses of ocean. Such figurative islands share many characteristics with actual island systems, in terms of unique plants and animals that are found there. One example is an inconspicuous plant named Smelowskia that inhabits alpine regions of the Pacific northwest. Smelowskia, named after the Russian botanist Timotheus Smelowsky (1770-1815), is found in northeast Asia and northwest North America, always near the summits of peaks that once protruded above the sea of ice. Such "islands" include Mt. Adams and Mt. Rainier in the Cascades, Mt. Stuart in the Stuart Range, Mt. Maude in the Entiat Range, North Navarre Peak in the Chelan Mountains, Old Baldy in the Okanogan Range, and Mt. Angeles and Mt. Constance in the Olympics. In several of its locations, Smelowskia shows slight differences in appearance—indicators of environmental conditions that vary slightly from place to place.

The most dramatic illustration of isolation and evolution at work in the mountain ranges comes when a new species is formed because conditions in the environment favor a particular set of inherited traits. A species or subspecies restricted to a specific range is called an "endemic." Many areas of Washington's mountains claim endemics, but several regions are especially rich. These include Mt. Rainier, the Wenatchee Mountains, the Blue Mountains, and the Olympics. Endemism is another sign that mountains create a multitude of conditions that foster great diversity among earth's living things.

Unseen by most of us, topographic relief establishes boundaries that shift imperceptibly as slow changes resonate through the environment. Our mountain ranges are the repositories of the tell-tale signs of these shifts. Guarded among the cirques and slopes of creeping talus, wedged into the frost-shattered boulders, preserved in the cold aeries and mountain haunts, are the signs of transitions, to which living cells, tissues and organisms have made adjustment. And the diversity which has yielded success. Mountains heighten differences among living things because they foster extremes in the conditions of life. They inhibit the even exchange of genetic material and they create conditions that not every organism can survive. Existence is played out dramatically in the world of rock, ice and thin air. Here growing seasons pass quickly, and competition for scarce resources is bitterly acute. Here, a novel twist in the strand of a gene may critically alter the physiology, appearance or behavior of an organism, suiting it better for its thin, mountain subsistence. Mountains, formed of great crustal blocks in motions that jar the earth, or exhaled as the fiery breath of the molten aquifers, leave their faint imprints in the cells of all their living inhabitants. Like mists, living tissues, organisms and populations mold themselves to the land's steep shoulders.

Left: E.B. Webster and the Olympic Mountain butterweed, or Webster's senecio, that he found. PORTRAIT COURTESY CLALLAM COUNTY HISTORICAL SOCIETY, PORT ANGELES; COLOR PHOTO COURTESY OF NATIONAL PARK SERVICE

Right: Charles V. Piper and the Piper's bellflower. PORTRAIT, NEG. NO. UW 2319, SPECIAL COLLECTIONS DIVISION, UNIVERSITY OF WASHINGTON LIBRARIES, SEATTLE; COLOR PHOTO BY PAT O'HARA

As late as 1890, rumors circulated about the mysteries locked deep in the the Olympic Mountains. One story had it that the mountain ramparts surrounded a large central valley, a magical Eden inhabited by animals and plants previously unknown to science. Expeditions were mounted in 1891 by the U.S. Army and a Seattle newspaper to explore the deep Olympic valleys and reveal the secrets of the unknown land.

The expeditions were successful. The interior was traversed and inspected, the blank space on the map etched with rivers and peaks. No great valley was discovered, and only a few new organisms were recorded. In the words of Prof. Louis Henderson, botanist with the Army expedition:

"I had hoped to excite envy in the breasts of many of my botanical friends by my rare 'finds.'...I had hoped to write a paper which should attract the notice of many scientific men to this flowery El Dorado; [instead] I find that I must content myself with the description of a flora trite in the extreme to those who are acquainted with the plants of the northwest."

Henderson's downcast mood may have been tempered when he did succeed in locating at least one species never previously collected or described. The disappointment he registered after his trip could only reflect the soaring expectations he carried with him at its outset.

The mountains of Washington contain numerous species unknown elsewhere. The Wenatchee Mountains, Mounts Adams and Rainier, the Blue Mountains and the Olympics all foster endemic forms—species or subspecies native to and limited to their restricted environs. Because they were explored relatively late, the Olym-

Left: J.B. Flett and Flett's violet. PORTRAIT COURTESY OLYMPIC NATIONAL PARK, PORT ANGELES; COLOR PHOTO BY TOM & PAT LEESON

Right: Louis F. Henderson and the Olympic rockmat (Petrophytum hendersoni). PORTRAIT COURTESY OF MRS. JEAN WALKINSHAW, SEATTLE; COLOR PHOTO COURTESY NATIONAL PARK SERVICE

pics—Henderson's remarks notwithstanding—were a fairly rich lode of undescribed species. Professional and amateur naturalists alike were able to engrave their latinized names on the pages of scientific journals.

Endemism in the Olympics is probably the result of populations that have shrunk and are now restricted to areas that remained exposed during periods of glaciation. Isolated from close relatives, plants and animals developed or lost various characteristics because of environmental conditions or because the normal assortment of genes within the population was altered as it got smaller. Actual evolutionary divergence is very difficult to identify, yet scientists have established that the Olympics have given rise to both animals and plants that are endemic to the isolated and only recently explored region.

Plants considered endemic in the Olympics include Webster's senecio, Flett's violet, Piper's bellflower, Olympic rockmat, Olympic aster, Olympic mountain daisy, Cotton's milkvetch, and several subspecies or varieties of other plants. Animals include the Olympic marmot, the Olympic chipmunk, the Olympic snow-mole and several subspecies of other mammals.

Mountain ranges often constitute biological islands. The dynamics of change in living things over time are dramatic and invite active investigation. The Olympics give us a glimpse of evolution in action—where separation and differentiation have been at work for eons. While it is no biologist's Valhalla, the mountain ranges do yield their surprises. And to the hardy observers who first ventured into their midst they held the opportunity for the naturalist's form of canonization—an organism bearing his own name.

CHAPTER FOUR

THE OLD CONTINENTAL RANGES

Short-tailed weasel. TOM & PAT LEESON

Sunrise in the Kettle Range. PAT O'HARA

The mountain landscape is beginning to show itself. Part of Washington state, admitted by its residents to be remote, is unfolding in a series of roadcuts and vistas of rolling terrain that darkens into rainclouds of the north. I stop to clamber over a roadside rock formation, to gain some perspective on a countryside unfamiliar to me. Serviceberries are bursting into bloom. The rose is familiar, likewise the lodgepole pine, Rocky Mountain juniper and the arrowleaf balsamroot. The fern, however, is new—and it's everywhere. Delicate knots of it grow out of the broken slabs of granite, from cracks and spaces between angular blocks.

Each frond is composed of tiny, serrated leaflet-like pinnae. Each tiny pinna has on its surface minute hairs and on the reverse, six or eight sori, the tiny dots that house spores. Keying the plant later, I learn that it is Woodsia scopulina, *Rocky Mountain woodsia. Its distribution, according to the books, is "widespread cordilleran., e. irreg. to Que." Cordillera, roughly translated, means "rope." We use it to mean "chain," and in this particular sense, "mountain chain." The cordillera is the backbone of the American continents and I, out of my own familiar coastal mountain range, am standing in it. Although just a few hundred miles from home, I might just as well be on the moon for the similarities that this fern habitat shares with fern habitats of the Olympics, the mountain range on the extreme western side of the state.*

Washington's northeastern ranges—the Selkirks and the Kettle—rise to the north of the aromatic steppes of bunchgrass and rabbitbrush that bake in the Eastern Washington sun. Hot basalt washes give way to parklands of ponderosa and quaking aspen. The land rises into rolling, larch-forested hills, which in turn become bare granite domes, layers peeling off like leaves of cabbage. The round forms continue to rise. Flat, glacial lake valleys narrow as the ridges steepen. Rivers gather in the north-lying creases, following the pathways abandoned with the retreat of the ice. Some, like the Pend Oreille, flow north. Others—the Columbia, the Colville, the Sanpoil and Kettle—flow south. Tributaries drain out of the parallel ridges, carving deep canyons in the ranges, gashes that reveal the inner rocks of a region of several major mountain- and continent-building events.

These ranges are not high by standards set farther west in the Cascades. Gypsy Peak and Abercrombie Mountain are the highest peaks, at 7,309' and 7,308' respectively. Because these ranges are older, time has left its rounding, gentling touch. Along the Kettle Crest, the elevation undulates around the 7,000' mark, the ridge easing along in a series of dips and climbs. It is country that rolls, steepening as you travel north, darkening, as pine forests merge with firs and spruces and as the canyons close. North, in Canada, all restraint is shed as the mountains become a jumble—ragged and untamed. Yet south of the border, along the Kettle Crest and atop other scattered peaks in the Selkirks, meadows appear more pastoral than alpine. Timberline is higher here than to the west, and the forests below are generally open. Where granite intrusions have been rubbed clean of glacial overburden, or where lightning has ignited ridgetop forests, wildflower communities thrive. High side valleys hold small lakes and ponds where beaver and muskrat thrive, wintering in mounded lodges of limbs and cattail stems. Moose, grizzly, and an occasional caribou have their haunts in these mountains, attesting to the principal regional affinity of the area to the Rocky Mountains.

The formation of these ranges is interpreted as a series of events in which the westward-moving North American continent bore the brunt of a collision with an exotic continental fragment being carried along on the eastward-moving oceanic plate. The old continent is in evidence as sedimentary layers found throughout the mountains

Old Continental Ranges

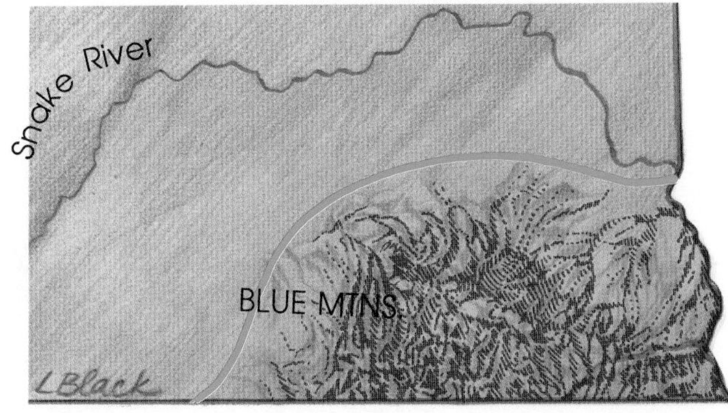

and a few outcrops of older, metamorphosed continental material.

In the east, along the Idaho border, fragments of the continent are composed of a formation found throughout the northern Rockies. This assemblage, called the Belt Supergroup, was laid along the continental margin as long ago as one billion years during an era called the Precambrian. There is no fossil record associated with the Belt sediments—emergent life was still brewing as primitive algaes and soft-bodied invertebrates.

In the Pend Oreille River Valley, massive Cambrian limestone deposits contain ores of lead and zinc. Northwest of Metaline, a Seattle City Light hydroelectric dam straddles a narrow gorge, its huge, whirring generators housed entirely in a vault carved into a limestone mountain. These limestones and associated sedimentary rocks formed as the continental shelf in a shallow Gulf of Mexico-like sea about 500 million years ago. A long period of relative quiet ensued, during which sediments flowed off the continent, gathering in a sea that was slowly narrowing as the continent inched toward a collision with the approaching Okanogan microcontinent. This formed a sequence of sediments known as the Kootenay Arc.

Sediments of the Kootenay Arc are now tightly folded. The old continental shelf became compressed into a narrowing band as the Okanogan country crowded against North America. Folded Kootenay sedimentary rocks are visible in the Kettle Falls and Colville areas.

Throughout the region, domes of granite bulge upward through their surrounding formations, signs of more recent volcanic activity contained within the much older rock. Mt. Spokane presents a classic example of this process. On a larger scale, the Kettle Range itself consists of a granitic batholith, the name given to large intrusive bodies. Volcanic activity between 160 and 80 million years ago injected massive globs of magma into older, emplaced material. Cooling slowly deep within the rock, minerals crystalized into the salt-and-pepper granular forms we recognize as granite. In the vicinity of these intrusions, schists and gneisses, heat- and pressure-altered rocks, show the effects of the cooking they underwent as the hot magma was forced into the surrounding sedimentary and older granitic rock. Eventually, the granite became exposed as the softer rock around it weathered and eroded away. Throughout the Selkirk and Kettle ranges, granite is common and its weathered crumbs

Facing page: From the rolling crest of the Kettle Range looking west. Gentle slopes and fire-bald mountaintops characterize this range—a smooth dome of granite with an affinity to lightning. PAT O'HARA

Left: Salmo Mountain. Washington's Selkirks are subdued in comparison to the Canadian portion of the range. Rounded in the south, they steepen to the north. Their worn appearance belies their ruggedness and isolation, however—moose, grizzly, wolf and mountain caribou make these mountains Washington's wildest. PAT O'HARA

Above: Snowshoe hare. ED WOLFF

Rocky Mountain elk, introduced from Yellowstone National Park in 1930 to ease overpopulation there, thrive in the Blue Mountains. ED WOLFF

form well drained soil associated with larch forest parklands.

Also conspicuous in the river valleys of these ranges are deposits of gravel left after the glaciers receded. Foothill topography along the southern boundaries of the northeastern mountainous region rises out of broad, flat valleys that were formed when glacial Lake Spokane covered the lowlands and backed up into the valleys. Glacial rounding has tempered the mountains, belying their true wildness.

The Blue Mountains

Only the northern slope of the Blue Mountains crosses the boundary between Oregon and Washington. Nevertheless, this range is one of the most exciting of all of the northwest ranges for the variety of information it yields about the geologic story of the Pacific Northwest. The Blue Mountain Province, the highland covering much of eastern Oregon, as well as parts of Idaho and Washington, encompasses Hells Canyon (the deepest gorge in North America), the John Day fossil beds, which contain evidence of climates and living creatures of millions of years ago, and the Wallowa Mountains, a glaciated environment during the last major Ice Age that, today, bears no rivers of flowing ice. In addition, the Blue Mountain Province is a major physiographic boundary separating the Columbia Plateau Province from the Basin and Range Province of Nevada and southeast Oregon.

Washington's Blues occupy the extreme southeast corner of the state, where the Snake River swings in a wide counter-clockwise semi-circle to join the Columbia. Oregon Butte, the highest peak of the range in Washington, rises 6,401 feet above the welter of ponderosa pine- and larch-covered ridges. In the protected habitat of the Wenaha-Tucannon Wilderness Area, remnants of the Blue Mountain herd of Rocky Mountain elk wander undisturbed, protected from logging and settlement. Transplanted from Yellowstone National Park in 1930 as a way of relieving starvation to the herds, they have adopted the new range and appear to be thriving. The Blue Mountain onion, originally collected from Weller's Butte, is endemic to the dry soil of the mountains, and is considered the only endemic plant from the Washington spur of the Blues.

Out of the mountains pour the Tucannon, Asotin, Pataha and Grande Rhonde rivers, carving away at loose slopes of talus and bedrock similar to that found throughout the Columbia Plateau. The area is known for its dike swarms, groups of volcanic fissures, believed to be one source of the basalt that flooded over much of the region between 25 and 15 million years ago. The Blue Mountains of Washington are composed mostly of basalt, but closer to the southerly heart of the range, a complex series of sedimentary layers, volcanic debris and metamorphosed rocks are exposed. Oregon's most famous fossil beds, formations in the John Day valley, lie amid the many distinct layers that have eroded out of the heart of the range.

GRIZZLY BEARS AND MOUNTAIN CARIBOU

The Selkirk Mountains jut into Washington in the state's extreme northeastern corner, an area with a human population density of about one person for every ten square miles (6,400 acres). Given the nature of that "extra" space—dense mountain forests, avalanche chutes, pristine river bottoms—the land is crucial habitat for two of Washington's most reclusive creatures—the grizzly bear and the mountain caribou.

Washington's grizzly population consists of between 25 and 30 animals. Sightings have occurred as far south as Newport, and west into Stevens County. The bears seldom wander far into Washington, preferring to stay in the remoteness of the northeastern corner, and roaming across the borders into Idaho and British Columbia. The grizzly's persistence in this corner of Washington (it once ranged throughout the state except on the Olympic Peninsula) is due to the presence of key elements of high-quality grizzly range and to a healthy population reservoir north of the border. Broad river valleys that grow rich with early foliage provide the bears with essential spring forage. In June, serviceberries are abundant at mid-elevation, providing another key seasonal staple. Between July and September, huckleberries ripen on the higher slopes, completing the seasonal cycle during which the animal accumulates the necessary fat reserves to weather the lean of winter.

The grizzly bear has been protected by law in Washington since 1969, when the state population was at a low of an estimated five or six animals. That legislation, coupled with federal protection under the Endangered Species Act and cooperation from Canadian wildlife agencies, has assured that habitat requirements for bears are met, and that one of the northern hemisphere's most stately predators remains part of the Washington mountain fauna.

The Selkirk herd of mountain caribou, 25 to 30 animals that wander freely across state and international boundaries, has been called "the ghosts of the Selkirks." Although biologists suspect that it was never a large herd, the relict population is dangerously near the brink of extinction. Four mature bulls—the most productive males in the herd—wander into Washington state during winter and early spring, preferring to stay above 4,500 feet of elevation where they feed on beard-like lichens that grow among the dense stands of old-growth subalpine fir and Engelmann spruce forests. In summer, the bulls rejoin the scattered cows and calves in British Columbia. The key component of caribou habitat present in Washington, but less prevalent elsewhere, appears to be an abundance of old-growth timber. Logging and road-building, which began encroaching on the upper elevation spruce/fir forests during the '50s, and wildfire have inflicted heavy losses to the habitat. The present "endangered" status of the herd has helped check habitat loss, but low natural reproduction among the caribou continues to hamper the herd's recovery. As with the grizzly, interstate and international cooperation among wildlife agencies has led to a recovery program that leaves even the experts optimistic.

Mountain caribou and grizzly bears are each connecting links, living reminders of a wild heritage that all North Americans share. But for the stronghold of the Selkirks, a range few Washingtonians know or claim, these animals would vanish from the Washington mountainscape. In the boreal forests and isolated valleys of the extreme northeast, the Selkirks shelter the ghosts, the grizzlies and a wilderness past that, once lost, will never be replaced.

Two species—grizzly bears (JESS LEE) *and mountain caribou* (© GARY BRAASCH), *one that once ranged over nearly all of Washington and one that probably never ventured beyond its present range in the state—cling tenuously to survival in Washington's Selkirk Mountains.*

CHAPTER FIVE

OKANOGAN COUNTRY

Ponderosa pine. TOM & PAT LEESON

The Methow Valley, in the heart of the Okanogan highlands, reveals the scooping and rounding of continental glaciation. JEFF GNASS

The evening was coming on strong, with squadrons of mosquitos and no-see-ums arriving in waves. I don't remember how many trout I'd caught, but I must have been satisfied, because I was quitting while there was still enough light to see the fly dimple the water. After retrieving the last cast, I stepped through the limbs of a cedar that sprawled across the riverbed. Something on the river changed. Moving upstream toward me was an acute "V," the wake of some living craft. At its apex was a head, eyes, ears and whiskers. I froze.

The beaver didn't sense my presense. It approached a gravel bar no more than ten feet away. Waddling out of the water, it shook its matted fur, sending a shower of droplets arcing off in every direction. The damp fur gathered in spikes. The beaver took to cleaning itself, balanced on its haunches and tail, scratching its body furiously. Poised in stillness, yet unbetrayed, I too began to itch. First it was a sympathetic itch. Then, I noticed that the mosquitos were landing in droves, on my arms, my hands, my face and neck. I longed to scratch with abandon, knowing that as much as a flinch would startle the animal and end our intimate encounter. The harder the beaver scratched, the more I itched, the more mosquitos seemed to land on my exposed skin. It was sublime torture. A shy animal, ten feet distant, unaware of my presence and I, suffering the edge of self-control so that I could prolong a rare opportunity to observe.

When I broke the silence with an exasperated howl and launched into a dance, the beaver vanished. Silently, quickly, it submerged itself in the water and glided downstream. Gone. Down the river, past the aspens flickering, the black cottonwood, the Douglas fir, the lodgepole pine. Beyond the evening insect swarms, pools of cold water, the blue reflections of old mountains as they gathered twilight.

East of the Cascade crest, a jumble of ranges and peaks break the horizon. You stand at some vantage and swear that the summits never stop. You survey a map and conclude that starting cross-country on a true-north course, you could eventually reach the Arctic, having crossed only one or two roads along the way. It is wild country in that it is big country. It's untamed and unpeopled. In even a slight breeze you hear the sound of emptiness, a roaring silence. If you think about it very long, it gives a sense of chilly solitude.

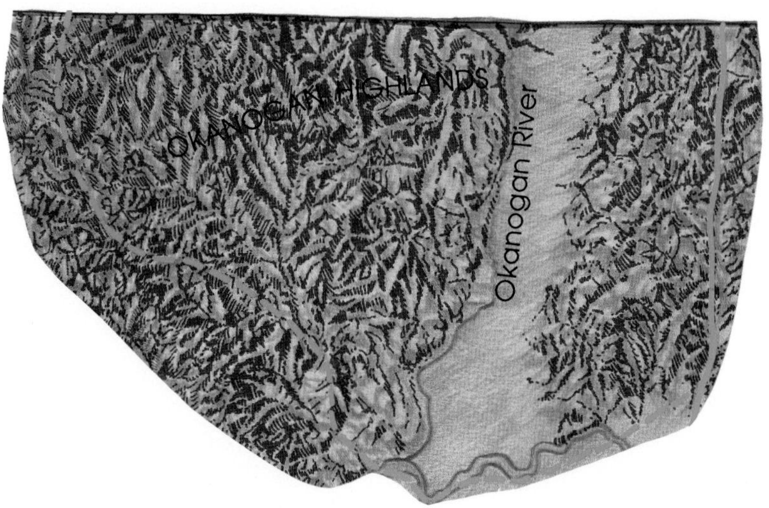

The country is Okanogan country. It's Pasayten country. It's country that bridges across Washington's top, anchored in the west to the North Cascades, in the east to the Kettles and Selkirks—the Rockies themselves. Dark peaks rise above avalanche-littered slopes. Fire-killed ghost forests straddle ridgelines. Thundershowers sweep down the valleys in the morning, back up in the afternoon. Cool mountain valleys hold their snowpack late. High lakes and streams sting with their chill even through the summer, the few brief weeks when the trails get dusty and yellowjackets prowl.

Geologically, the country between Republic and the Methow Valley is composed of remnants of two major continent-building episodes. The first, the docking of the Okanogan sub-continent, is thought to have occurred sometime about 100 million years ago. The second, the arrival of the leading edge of the North Cascades sub-continent, about 50 million years ago.

As the westward-moving North American plate approached an offshore island mass, referred to as the Okanogan sub-continent, the shallow sea lying between

Ancient sediments gently wrap a flower blossom—Okanogan country's complex geology yields the secrets of time itself. KARNA ORSEN

Kangaroo Ridge (left) and Early Winter Spires and Liberty Bell (opposite) are composed of some of the youngest granitic rock found in Washington, the Golden Horn Batholith. Frost has had a field day with the Golden Horn—wedging away great flakes to form pinnacles that puncture the sky, and walls that awe.
JEFF GNASS PHOTOS

them narrowed. The sediments of that sea are known as the Kootenay Arc. Kootenay sediments were folded and are present near the surface in the vicinity of Kettle Falls. The Okanogan sub-continent itself extends through the region infused with granite in the Kettle Range and west, to the Okanogan Valley. Geologists consider the Okanogan Valley to be the remnant of the old subduction trench formed after the addition of the Okanogan sub-continent, when the collision with the North Cascades sub-continent was imminent.

Between the Okanogan and Methow Rivers lies the leading edge and continental shelf of another continental mass, the North Cascades sub-continent, that collided with the growing margin of the North American plate. This collision brought two continental masses together and choked off the subduction process under the Okanogan sub-continent, leading to the end of volcanic activity that produced massive deposits of igneous andesite and rhyolite found in the Sanpoil Valley, south of Republic.

Major fault zones found north and west of the Methow Valley form the boundaries of the Methow Graben, a block of the North Cascades sub-continent that dropped. The graben itself consists of largely sedimentary rock, a series thought to be between 130 and 65 million years old. The northern fault, the Pasayten Fault, marks a hydrographic divide between the Methow River, a tributary of the Columbia, and the three forks of the north-flowing Pasayten River, a tributary of the Fraser. East of the Pasayten drainage, the Chewack flows southward, parallel to the Okanogan River.

Laced throughout the overall structure of the region are intrusions of granite and granodiorite, forced into the surrounding country about 60 million years ago. In some cases, younger intrusions have been emplaced within older intrusions, as in the case of the Golden Horn Batholith, which was forcefully injected into the older Black Peak intrusion. The Golden Horn Batholith includes Silver Star Mountain (8,876'), northwest of Winthrop. Much of the western region of the old Okanogan sub-continent also consists of granitic intrusions that formed a large erosion-resistant dome. Where the hot

Above: Mountain goats—uncommon and wary throughout their natural range in Washington. ED WOLFF
Right: The wolverine is a wilderness wanderer whose fearsome habits earn it respect from human visitors to its mountain hold. Largest of the weasel family, it is uncommon in Washington. JESS LEE

Facing page: Horseshoe Basin, in the Pasayten Wilderness. PAT O'HARA

magma contacted its enclosing material, it heated and altered the material. Often this has resulted in the formation of ore bodies within the zone of contact metamorphism. Famous mining areas, such as the Slate Creek and Conconully districts, are located in proximity to contact zones between intrusions and their surrounding country.

In more recent times, glaciers have scoured the region. One particularly vivid glacial landscape lies within the Methow Valley. Kame terraces, debris heaped along the flanks of a living glacier and stranded after the glacier melts, are visible throughout the lower reaches of the Methow Valley. Cirques, hanging valleys and moraines texture the more mountainous areas.

Interior regions of the Pasayten Wilderness reveal considerable erosive action made by large sheets of ice that covered significant portions of the high country. Northern faces of Mt. Lago (8,595'), Mt. Carru (8,745') and Osceola Peak (8,587') are deeply faceted while their southern flanks incline more gently. Glaciers that quietly waste in the shade of the Lago-Osceola ridge represent the easternmost in Washington—distance from the ocean and scant precipitation create a poverty diet.

Much of the high country of the Pasayten/Okanogan region consists of broad valleys and gently rolling shoulders. In lower reaches of the rivers, relief steepens as the cutting action responsible for the shape of the land is predominantly that of water. The Lost River canyon, draining the south-central Pasayten Wilderness, is a good example—the stream rises in open, glacier-carved country, and drops into its steep, untrailed canyon for its final descent to the Methow River.

As with its glaciers, Okanogan country lifeforms reflect certain continental associations. Precipitation is slight, often averaging 16 inches per year. High cirque basins foster picturesque stands of the deciduous conifer alpine larch—their needles iridescent green in early summer, transforming into flame yellow as autumn frost arrives. Ridges support generous stands of whitebark pine, Engelmann spruce and subalpine fir. Lower in the river valleys, lodgepole pine chokes alluvial flats, thick as dog hair.

Wildlife of the region includes much of the wildlife found in other Pacific Northwest mountain regions. Large mammals included the mountain goat, mule and white-tailed deer, black bear, cougar, lynx, bobcat and porcupine. Scattered herds of bighorn sheep are found in the area, mostly the product of reintroductions after native populations were wiped out early in the settlement era. Fur-bearers are common, including the beaver, marten, otter and, occasionally, the wolverine. Mountain bluebirds are common in parkland meadow areas, Clark's nutcracker in whitebark pine forests.

The country is a skier's dream in winter—cold and clear. In the Pasayten country, remote areas like Horseshoe Basin are tempting to the winter wilderness visitor. The relatively gentle slopes and stable climatic conditions minimize avalanche risk. Where local relief is pronounced, avalanches leave tell-tale signs, such as pick-up-stick jumbles of downed trees and open, rock-strewn meadows lining steep gullies.

The mountains of north-central Washington convey a peculiar remoteness. They receive less visitation and a different style of visitor than the mountains closer to civilization's door. They are the country of the horse-hunter, the fly fisherman, the pack-trip dude and wrangler. The hardware-toting alpinist, the mile-hungry backpacker, the wilderness visitor accustomed to the lushness and ease of other ranges, will be changed by this country. Among summits separated by greater distances, ridgelines uncomplicated by the aretes and gendarmes of more complex mountainscapes, land pale green and vast, this wilderness teaches lessons of breadth. The wild takes the form of distance. Its sensation is unsettling.

Wet rock glistens in the dayless world of a mineshaft. Slate Creek District mines rewarded a few for their luck, a few for their labor.
JACK HARRIS COLLECTION, TWISP, WASHINGTON

Throughout the period of exploration by military expeditions seeking wagon routes and intrepid settlers seeking land, Washington's mountains were scoured for mineral treasures. Early shows of coal in the Puget lowlands and the hopes of precious ores locked deep in the wilderness lured thousands of men up the writhing river valleys, seeking fortune, literally in the innards of the mountains.

Tributaries of the Skagit River showed early promise, with placer claims staked near the confluence of Ruby Creek and the Skagit River. Unsatisfied with pickings in the lower drainage of Ruby Creek, Alex Barron moved deeper into the wild country, tracking traces of placer gold that were attached to flecks of quartz. The trail led up Slate Creek, to Benson Mountain. No outcrops broke the surface, but after several test pits were dug, a quartz seam was located. Confident that he had found the source, he staked several claims high on the slopes of Benson Mountain. One Barron claim, the Eureka, proved very rich. Indeed, it consisted of seams of rotted quartz peppered with gold, buried under four to eight feet of soil and compressed, iron-stained clay. A patch of overlying debris measuring 30 by 40 feet was stripped, exposing the seam, and work began in earnest extracting the free gold.

Barron worked the vein for a time, then sold his claim to an Anacortes firm incorporating itself as the Eureka Mining Company for a sum between $50,000 and $80,000. The Eureka operation eventually earned its owners over $300,000. For Barron, however, the resulting wealth was short-lived. According to Joann Roe, in her book *The North Cascadians,* Barron "spent his poke in riotous living," and left the area for a while. A contemporary account, *Mining in the Pacific Northwest,* written by L.K. Hodges, reports Barron and two partners later returned, staking claims called the Beck Group, three miles up the valley.

The Beck claims, too, proved rich. Again, seams of quartz were found, dipping deep into the mountain. Hodges reported that, "The quartz shows from three to six feet in width, with a slate footwall, and porphyry in places on the hanging wall. The quartz is generally white, carrying very little oxide of iron. It carries gold, silver and a small quantity of copper, an average of four assays giving 2 3/4 ounces gold and 51 ounces silver."

Barron's fortunes again soared. According to Roe, his new operation left him between $75,000 and $100,000 richer.

Meanwhile, the Eureka operation pressed deeper into its quartz vein. In 1895, a five-by-nine-foot shaft descended 54 feet into the mountain—ore had to be hoisted

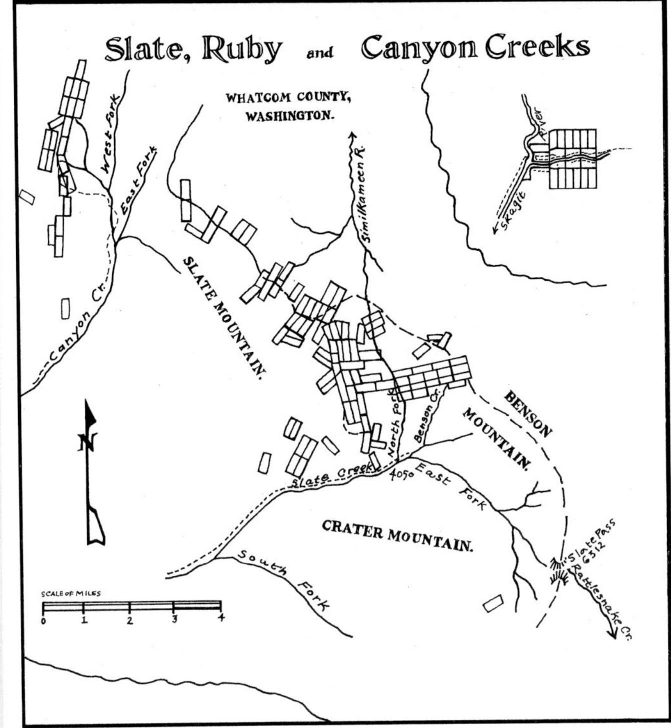

The neat subdivisions of the claims map belied the ruggedness of the land; the town of Barron enjoyed no such dominance over its topography. The land eventually won. PHOTO COURTESY OF UNIVERSITY OF WASHINGTON

out of the hole by hand. Other tunnels were carved into the vein from lower on the slope, each one encountering the rich quartz as it dipped into the very foundation of the mountain.

The Eureka's success proved to be a magnet to other prospectors and their entourages. The town of Barron, founded in 1900, flourished, with a population near 2,500, high in the valley above Slate Creek. In all, over 80 claims were actively worked in the Slate Creek District during the 1890s. Access was poor, the nearest railhead being at what is now Sedro Woolley, nearly 90 miles to the west. A road extended as far as Marblemount and a trail, perched tenuously above the Skagit Gorge, continued to Ruby Creek, where a bustling settlement thrived. Another 25 miles of trail wound into the Slate Creek country. To the east, a trail extended over Slate Pass (now Hart's Pass), into the upper Methow drainage. The trail clung to the side of the canyon for 15 miles where it met the road leading down the Methow Valley to the Columbia River at Ives Landing (now Brewster), 75 miles distant.

The heyday of Barron was short. Distance from smelters and a need for good roads plagued the mines and the boomtown they created. In time, miners and their echelons of camp-followers moved on; avalanches and underbrush reclaimed the mountainside that fortune briefly visited.

CHAPTER SIX

THE CASCADES

Columbine. PAT O'HARA

Right: the Picket Range. PAT O'HARA

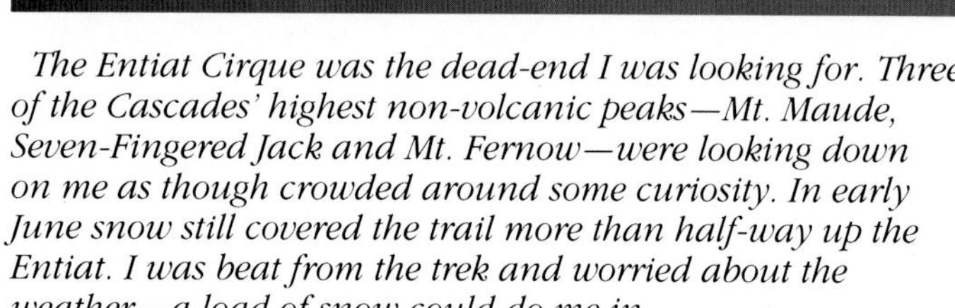

The Entiat Cirque was the dead-end I was looking for. Three of the Cascades' highest non-volcanic peaks—Mt. Maude, Seven-Fingered Jack and Mt. Fernow—were looking down on me as though crowded around some curiosity. In early June snow still covered the trail more than half-way up the Entiat. I was beat from the trek and worried about the weather—a load of snow could do me in.

I climbed up off the sloping floor of the cirque basin to a patch of subalpine fir and spread my sleeping bag in a little trough between hummocks of heather. I ate hurriedly and crawled into the bag. Overhead, clouds looked like the undersides of ships' hulls. They stretched from one close horizon to the other. Hunkering down into the bag I hoped for the best and quickly was asleep.

When I awakened, the sky ships were gone. It was still evening and it was not clear by the neutrality of shade whether the sky was thick with overcast or clear. Between light of day and dark of night there was twilight ("between light"). Its ambiguity played equally on hope and dread. No stars showed. Then from the forest below came a lilting tone. A varied thrush gave its eerie, solitary call, a flatted third to an unsung tonic—a minor chord somehow embodied in a single note. Above one of Seven-Fingered Jack's stumpy digits the evening star switched on in the west. The sky, I decided, was clear.

The Cascades Range has many such dead ends, many haunting cirques, places where the stir of a birdsong, the echo of a falling rock or the groan of wind conjures deep feelings in a solitary visitor. It is the nature of wilderness to evoke in us sensations unknown in the press of company, the lap of relative luxury, the midst of our civilized world. "Wild" is indeed synonymous with "Cascades."

The Cascades of this chapter are the peaks and formations from the Canadian border to the Columbia River that are not recently formed by volcanic processes. They are the Stuarts, the Pickets, the Tatooshes, the Chilliwacks. They are big blocks of the Bonanza group, the Cascade Crest massif, The Pride of the Mountains Ridge. They are the mountains called Terror, Perdition, Isolation and Fury; or The Chisel, Bear's Breast and Sharkfin Tower. They are mountains which, as descriptive names suggest, convey vivid images and reveal odd associations—their pull at human imagination.

The Cascade Range is anchored at its southern end in northern California, dominated for its first several hundred miles of length by its volcanoes. Broadly spaced volcanic peaks perch on the Oregon Cascade Crest, rising above the rolling terrain like cairns on a trailless meadow. The uplift is particularly noticeable where the Columbia River has filed a neat groove through the mountains along the Columbia Gorge, keeping an even pace with the arch-building process that raises the land, on an average, 4,000 feet above sea-level.

North, into Washington, the divide steepens. Rainier, St. Helens and Adams still dominate the horizon, like islands, yet broken land rises out of the forested highlands in larger, more closely spaced patches. It's like a storm brewing on the ocean. The trend continues north, as the surrounding formations begin to swallow even the big volcanoes. In the North Cascades, the range has reached full boil. The land's fury is that of a gale. Frothy summits are whitecaps. The islands seem to founder amid a turbulent sea of peaks.

Geologically, the pre-Quaternary Cascades are complex. Until recently, the Cascades were thought to be the result of a mountain-building process known as a geosyncline. This theory, which predates theories of plate tectonics and terrane accretion, holds that sediments accumulate in a deep trough, forced downward over many millions of years by the increasing sediment load.

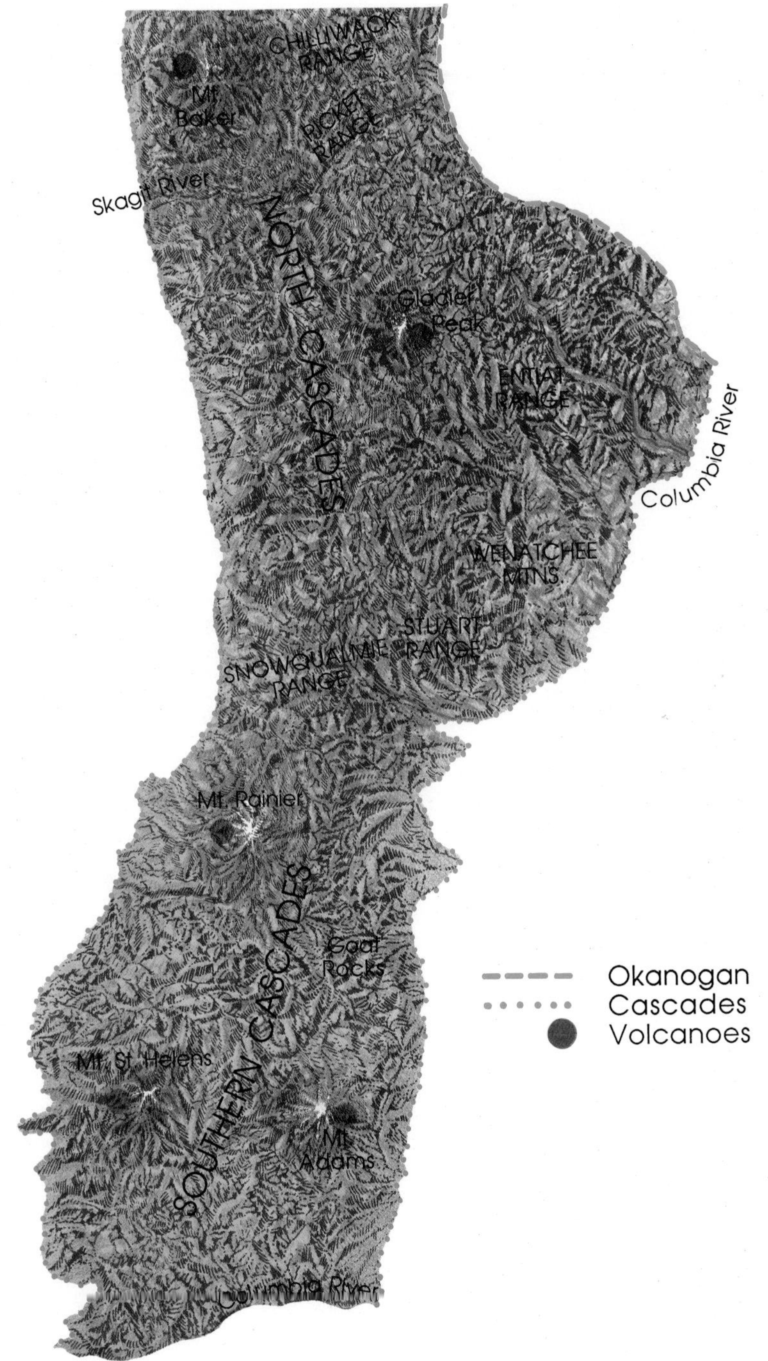

Above: Glacier Peak (10,541') viewed from Evergreen Mountain. Right: Lake Chelan, a landlocked fjord carved by a massive river of ice, stretches 55 miles—from the heart of the North Cascades to the dry sage hills of the Columbia Basin. Facing page: Boulder River high country, wilderness within sight of the Sound. PAT O'HARA PHOTOS

Eventually, pressure generated by the sediment burden generates heat, giving rise to volcanic activity. Such volcanism, the theory goes, alters accumulated sediments by heating, crystallization and deformation. The result is a crystalline backbone that forms the central core of a mountain range. Massive formations of sedimentary rock lie to either side of the crystalline core, upturned and broken in the mountain-building event.

While most of the components that would suggest a geosynclinal mountain-building episode are present in the North Cascades, the general utility of the theory itself has been eclipsed by the more powerful mechanisms of plate tectonics and terrane theory. Volcanism itself is much better explained by the process of subduction and the movement of plates—in fact, volcanism created simply by downwarping pressure, as postulated in the geosyncline theory, has not actually been detected operating anywhere on earth.

According to Alt and Hyndman, much of the country now part of the Cascade Range was once an island, much like Borneo, New Zealand or Japan. Within the island, volcanic processes worked, driven by subduction that was occurring off the island's west coast. Sea floor and North American continental movement carried the island subcontinent to our vicinity, plastering it against the what now is the Okanogan Highland. More deformation resulted as the exotic landscape collided with the leading edge of North America. Volcanoes on the now-anchored island continued to erupt, creating a platform often referred to as the western Cascades.

Uplift and compression have broken large fragments of that island continent into a melange of large formations, tilted and turned, and bearing on one another along well defined fault systems. Magma injections have blistered the ancient formations with large domes of granite. Pressure and heat, at work for perhaps hundreds of millions of years, have altered many rocks metamorphically, creating a large region of schists and gneisses, products of such deep earth forces, and the "core" of the Cascades.

It is possible to break the pre-Quaternary Cascades into two general provinces, corresponding to rock types that are revealed in each. Such a distinction recognizes a simple visual impression of differences between the rugged North Cascades and the more recumbent Southern Cascades.

The North Cascades

In 1882, Lieutenant Henry H. Pierce led a successful exploring expedition across what we now call Cascade Pass, in the North Cascades. It was not entirely enjoyable. Perched high in the Stehekin Canyon, after ferrying horse loads on their own backs, the party settled down for the night. "The sleet continuing, and the bundles already saturated, few blankets were spread," Pierce wrote.

"During the night the sleet became snow, and, what with the weirdlike darkness, the thunder of falling masses of ice into the neighboring canyons, the ceaseless roar of the torrents, and the howling of the wind, the situation was rendered dismal beyond description."

Enough said, except that when first light appeared, it was still snowing and the party was without breakfast or even a coffee pot. Pierce's assessment of the route in his report to General Nelson A. Miles was terse: "Beyond the crossing of the Twitsp [Twisp River], the route passed over from Colville to the Sound should in no way be recommended, nor is there, in my judgement, likely to arise any military necessity for its use west of that point."

Left: Miles of vacant space separates Image Lake from seemingly touchable Glacier Peak. PAT O'HARA

Routes through the mountains would later be developed in passes that afforded more breathing room and less grade. It was not until 1972 that a road linked east and west sides of the North Cascades. Until that time, motorists and freight used routes considerably farther south at Stevens and Snoqualmie passes. Landform features that have posed these obstacles are caused by the region's extreme relief, caused by a combination of glacier and water erosion.

The North Cascades receive abundant precipitation. Snowpack and runoff can both be quite high, resulting in complex hanging, cirque and valley glacier systems and deeply incised drainages. Add to this the presence of numerous discrete blocks of relatively hard rock—granitic intrusions and chunks of the metamorphic core of the range—and the result is steeply towering peaks, heavily sculpted along their flanks, and deeply eroded canyons.

Of the approximately 1,100 glaciers found in the lower 48 United States, the North Cascades alone can claim at least 750. Glaciation has worked the range hard and remains an active force shaping the land. Glaciers also create much of the visual drama in this environment of extreme contrasts.

Naming principal peaks of the region is like a "Who's Who" of Washington mountains. Picturesque Shuksan (9,127'), remote Bonanza Peak (9,511'), pyramidal Goode (9,200'), and inscrutable Redoubt (8,956') are just the beginnings of the list that crown this spectacular part of the Cascades. Great climbs like the overhanging North Wall of Bear, the Picket Traverse, and the Nooksack Tower, are the topics of innumerable between-trip conversations of diehard Washington climbers.

The faint blush of alpenglow settles over Mt. Shuksan (9,127'). PAT O'HARA

Ptarmigan Traverse

Left: Dome Peak (8,920+'), which the party traversed on July 21, 1938, the first day of serious climbing.
Right: Mt. Formidable (8,325'), their second first-ascent of the trip, which was made July 25. BOB AND IRA SPRING PHOTOS

The summer of 1938 was a summer bone dry and pistol hot in the North Cascades. And for a loose confederation of young Seattle climbers who called themselves "Ptarmigans," the summer of '38 was to become legend for other reasons. The Great Depression was in full swing, jobs were hard to come by and for Calder Bressler, Ray Clough, Tom Myers and Bill Cox, no work and less money meant just one thing—go climbing.

The group had grown up climbing together as Boy Scouts. When Scout headquarters disavowed their increasingly harrowing exploits they formed the Ptarmigan Climbing Club. As Ptarmigans, they launched outings and expeditions throughout the Cascades and Olympics and steadily honed the individual and collective skills that would earn them a startling array of first and second ascents.

They left their most indelible mark along the jagged crest of the Cascades between Dome Peak and Cascade Pass, a route now called, in their honor, the Ptarmigan Traverse. On July 18, 1938, Ptarmigans Bressler, Clough, Myers and Cox left Seattle in a Model A, headed for the Suiattle River Valley and the Cascades' inner sanctum. The plan of action was to thread along the Cascade Crest and climb everything along the route. Four major groups of peaks lay between Dome and Cascade Pass, each separated by a day's trek over glaciers, meadows, cirque basins and thin-edged ridges.

On July 21, the party made the first traverse of Dome

Peak and the second ascent of Spire Point. On July 23, the party trekked for half the day, climbed Sentinel Peak, Old Guard and "sauntered" to the top of LeConte Mountain, a first ascent that left the group, in Bressler's words, "exhilerated by the novelty." On July 25, the group took on Mt. Formidable and Spider Mountain and as Bressler wrote, "since Magic [Mountain] happened to be above us just to the east, in the long afternoon shadows we ran up it and down it." All three were firsts.

The next day the Ptarmigans followed a mountain goat to the summit of Johannesburg Mountain, then bivouacked high on the massive, dark-walled, ice-spitting monster of a peak. After a day back in camp resting, the four climbed Sahale and Boston peaks and Mt. Buckner, choosing, after the Buckner ascent, to call the northward march quits—not enough Tricouni nails remained in all of their boots to outfit a single safe boot. More by trail than alpine traverse, the Ptarmigans returned to the waiting Model A, thirteen days, six first ascents, and four second ascents later. Fourteen years would pass before the feat was repeated. Today, approaches to the route are easier but the classic alpine traverse is undertaken only infrequently. Access and notoriety notwithstanding, the Ptarmigan remains formidable—those who try it leave with new respect for its youthful pioneers.

Left: Magic Mountain (7,610'), another of the Ptarmigans' first ascents, was bagged on July 25. Right: The view from Magic's summit toward Johannesburg Mountain (third peak along ridge, 8,200+'), a first ascent made July 26.
BOB AND IRA SPRING PHOTOS

Mt. Index (5,979') towers above the Skykomish River—local relief, and not overwhelming height, makes Index one of the most breathtaking peaks in the central Cascades. PAT O'HARA

Southern Cascades

Although the topography gives the appearance of spreading out somewhat in the southern Cascades, the mountainscape is by no means tame. Glaciation has been less intense, owing to lower latitude and base elevation, and therefore erosion has been somewhat less instrumental in sculpting the land. Predominant rocks of the Cascades south of Stevens Pass differ from those north. Instead of intensely altered metamorphics common through the northern part of the range, southern Cascade rocks consist more of volcanics formed in the last 15 million years and intrusive bodies less than 60 million years of age. Batholiths found in this region include the Tatoosh and Bumping Lake plutons, near Mt. Rainier, and the Snoqualamie, Index, Grotto and Stuart batholiths farther north along the crest.

An area of significant geologic and biological significance is the Stuart Range of the Wenatchee Mountains. Quartz-diorite in composition, the Stuarts represent the exposed roof of a once-enclosed mass of magma that cooled slowly and formed distinct crystals. Mt. Stuart, at 9,415 feet, dominates the range, surrounded by lesser summits in the spectacular group. Scrubbed granite basins in the range bear startling similarities to the High Sierra, a likeness uncommon between the Cascades and the California range. The Alpine Lakes Wilderness Area now encloses much of the Stuart Range, guarding the unique region from development and despoliation.

Of botanical significance is the presence of serpentine soils in areas of the Wenatchee Mountains. For a mountain region as connected to other mountainous areas as the Wenatchees are, an unusually high incidence of endemic plants is noted.

Peaks of the Snoqualmie Pass vicinity are for many Washington visitors and residents the most accessible and visible of all Washington's non-volcanics. The group is dominated by Mt. Snoqualmie (6,278') and Kaleetan and Chair peaks (6,259' and 6,238', respectively). Local relief accounts for much of these peaks' spectacular scenic character—they tower an average of 4,000 feet above the hissing traffic of Interstate 90.

The Snoqualmie Batholith represents one of several zones of granitic intrusion in the central portion of the Cascades, emplaced probably within the last 20 million years. Neighboring batholiths include the Grotto and

Mt. Stuart and Stuart Lake in the Alpine Lakes Wilderness. The Stuart Range has been called "Washington's Sierras." PAT O'HARA

Washington's southern Cascades. View across American Ridge, in the Cougar Lakes Wilderness, to Mt. Adams. PAT O'HARA

Right: Goat Rocks Wilderness and Mt. Adams.
Below: The Stuarts.
Facing page: Crystal Lake and Enchantment Basin in Alpines Lakes Wilderness.
PAT O'HARA PHOTOS

Index plutons that lie just north of the Snoqualmie intrusion. The Index structure is well represented in the massive multiple spires of Mt. Index (5,979'), just south of where U.S. Highway 2 climbs toward Stevens Pass. Here again, vigorous glacial and stream erosion and relatively hard peaks create stark contrast in elevation between the peaks and valleys—the local relief is breathtaking. Contact metamorphism—the heating and subsequent alteration of parent country by the forceful injection of magma—has created many ore pockets adjacent to all of these batholiths. Prospecting and mining, although now uncommon, represented the first chapters of white settlement of this region of the Cascades.

The Tatoosh Pluton and its representative peaks in the Mt. Rainier area often go unnoticed because they are so powerfully overshadowed by the big volcano itself. They would, however, provide spectacular enough scenery and geologic interest, without Rainier, to deserve mention and their fair share of credit. The Tatoosh Pluton actually forms the footing upon which Rainier itself rests.

During the Miocene and Pliocene epochs (between 25 and 3 million years ago), activity was intense, as magma surged into older igneous and sedimentary formations. Exploiting cracks and joints in the overlying rocks, Tatoosh granodiorite filled available spaces like frosting between cake layers, resulting in many dikes and sills visible today among older rocks. In addition, andesite lavas forming the Palisades, just south of Rainier, are thought to have been surface flows of the Tatoosh magma that was elsewhere contained underground. Other exposures of the Tatoosh Pluton are found east and north of the volcano that grew upon it in areas where the mantle that once covered the batholith has eroded away.

South of Rainier, the Old Cascades make fewer dramatic appearances—forests cloak the gentling terrain and the recent cones of St. Helens and Adams attract the eye. In a last major show of scenic splendor, the old rocks show their head—spectacularly—as Goat Rocks.

Goat Rocks are the remnants of a Cascade stratovolcano that lived and died between 15 and 2 million years ago. Mt. Gilbert Curtis is the highest peak of the group, at 8,201 feet. The Goat Rocks group hugs the Cascade Crest as a gently arcing ridge, glaciated on its north and east slopes. Erosion has worked the Goats over intensely, revealing remnants of the once-mighty volcano's central vent in Black Thumb (approx. 7,750 feet).

The Goat Rocks area is one of Washington's oldest wilderness areas, designated by the U.S. Forest Service as the Goat Rocks Primitive Area in 1931. Sparse vegetation yields excellent vantages of Cascade volcanoes that rise above the rolling hills; Mt. Adams, Mt. Rainier and Mt. St. Helens are palpably near; hazy forms of Hood and other distant Cascades roll off the horizon.

CHAPTER SEVEN

THE OLYMPICS

Autumn in Olympic National Park. TOM & PAT LEESON

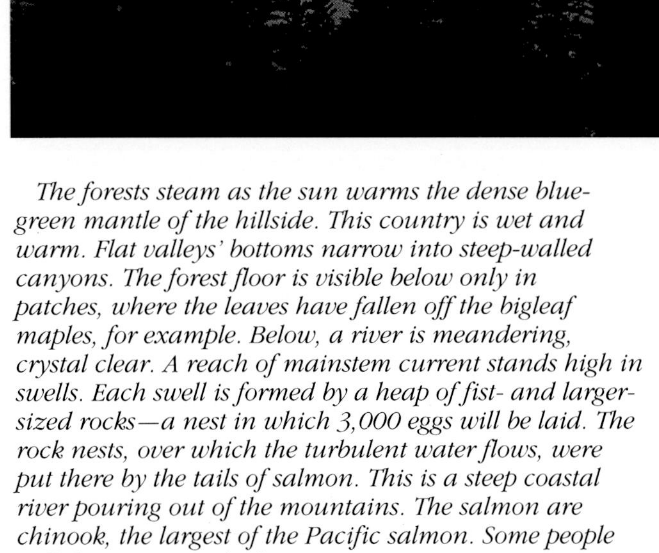

Right: Clouds over Olympic National Park from Deer Park. TOM & PAT LEESON

The forests steam as the sun warms the dense blue-green mantle of the hillside. This country is wet and warm. Flat valleys' bottoms narrow into steep-walled canyons. The forest floor is visible below only in patches, where the leaves have fallen off the bigleaf maples, for example. Below, a river is meandering, crystal clear. A reach of mainstem current stands high in swells. Each swell is formed by a heap of fist- and larger-sized rocks—a nest in which 3,000 eggs will be laid. The rock nests, over which the turbulent water flows, were put there by the tails of salmon. This is a steep coastal river pouring out of the mountains. The salmon are chinook, the largest of the Pacific salmon. Some people call them "tyee"—the kings.

Chinook salmon are fish of mountain rivers. Their earthly haunts are coastal river systems that circle the north Pacific. Genetically endowed for swift current and large cobble bottoms, chinook are nature's answer to the challenge to populate an explosively unstable environment with the substance of flesh. Broad and muscular, chinook thrash up the flooding canyons, deposit their eggs in the shade of overhanging canyon walls and die. As much as any creature that spends up to four-fifths of its life roaming the ocean, chinook salmon represent mountainous country. Young, mountainous country. Country that rings with the sound of gulls; where ocean fogs condense on the needles of dripping conifers.

Washington's youngest mountain region is its coastal range. North, the Olympics Mountains rake the horizon in a dramatic study of uplift and deformation. South of the Chehalis River, the Willapa Hills rise, blue rolling hills, a lower topography, but structurally and geographically related to the Olympics. Together, they form a mountain belt, capturing wet winds just in from the ocean, shedding a handful of chinook-bearing rivers—the Elochoman, the Naselle, the Chehalis, Humptulips, Hoh, Queets and Calawah. The Elwha. The others.

The jury is still out on the precise mechanism that formed Washington's coast range, yet agreement prevails over the general outline of their origin. Within 300 miles off the coast of Washington, the earth's crust is splitting and new magma is rising through the fissure to become sea floor. To either side of the rift a lip of new crust is being formed, where older crust is carried away from the split. Thus, the sea floor spreads, riding a great crustal conveyor belt of convection currents in the earth's mantle, which delivers the ocean floor to the continent's doorstep. Upon this conveyor belt are the remains of what was once an underwater mountain range of volcanoes.

Basalt, the dark, dense lava formed in submarine volcanic eruptions, forms vast wedges, partly interleaved with ocean sediments shed from the pre-Olympic continental edge of North America. Caught on the leading edge of a westward-moving North America, like snow on a snow-shovel, basalt and marine sediments are an upturned jumble. The mountains are that heap.

The Willapa Hills form the gently rising landscape bounded by the Columbia River on the south, the Cowlitz River on the southeast and the Chehalis River on the east and north. Although they bear very little resemblance to the Olympics, the Willapa Hills are structurally closely related, being composed of sea floor volcanics of similar age. Recent theorists consider basalts of the Willapa Hills region to be part of the southward extension of basalts found in the Olympics and part of the sea floor that was not drawn under the continent's edge in the subduction process. Boistfort Peak, at 3,110', is the highest peak of the heavily forested (and heavily logged) region.

Geologists long puzzled over the curious amalgam of rocks in the Olympic Mountains themselves. To the west, along the coast and protruding into the heart of the mountains, are sedimentary rocks—sandstones, slates and shales. Wrapped around the sedimentary rocks like a horseshoe, its open end facing west, is the Crescent For-

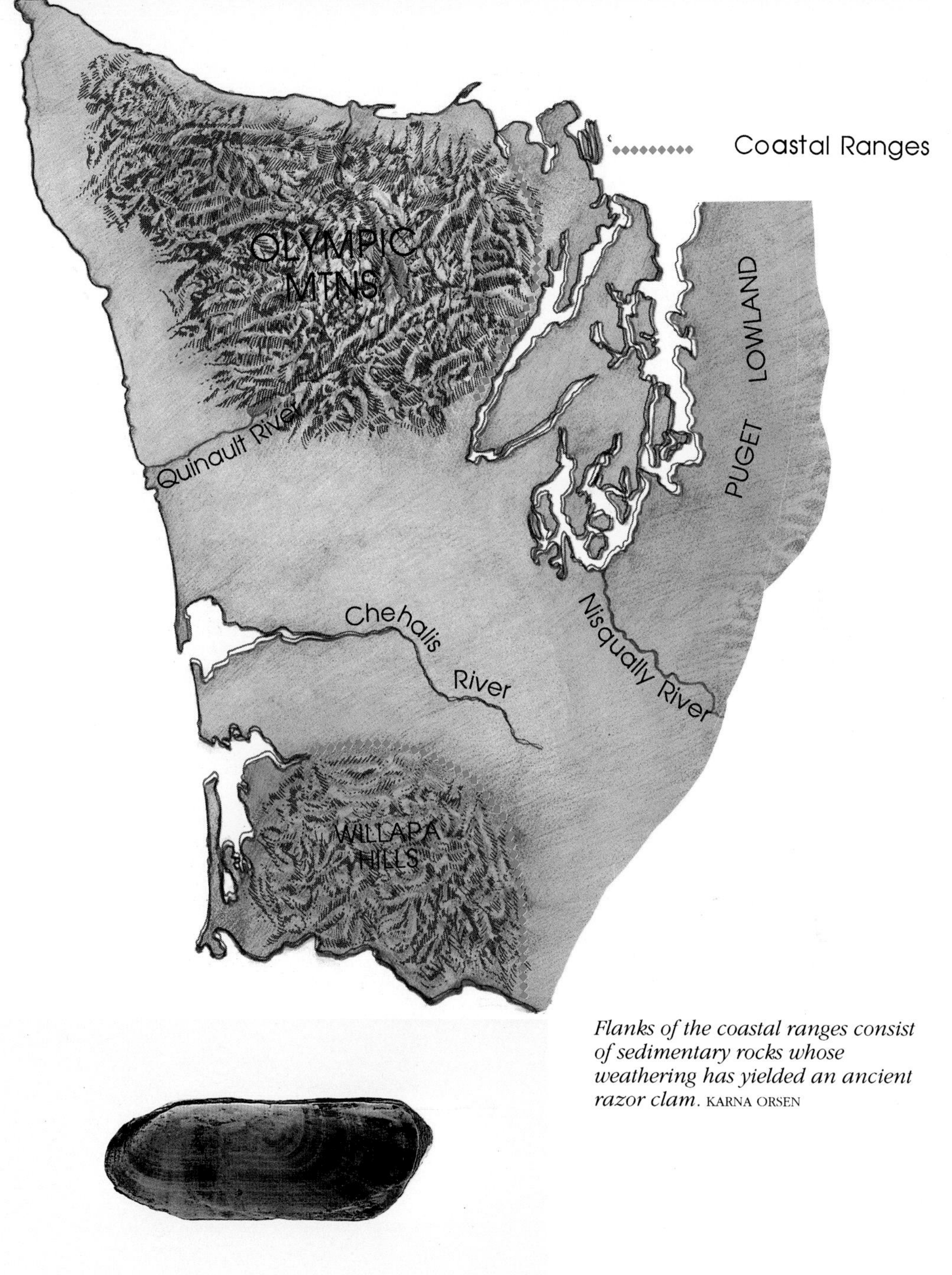

Flanks of the coastal ranges consist of sedimentary rocks whose weathering has yielded an ancient razor clam. KARNA ORSEN

mation—basalt, tipped on edge and warped from relentless tectonic forces.

Mt. Olympus is the highest peak in the coastal province, reaching 7,965'. Although it dominates surrounding peaks and is visible from sea, Olympus would be lost if uprooted and transplanted amid the Cascades. It owes its drama to extremely variable weather, proximity to the ocean, and a complex mantle of glaciers that cloak its flanks and which have carved its multiple summit horns. Composed of crumbling sandstone interbedded with slate, Olympus sediments are considered slightly younger than those of the basalt horseshoe. This evidence helped steer theorists away from an earlier belief that the horseshoe formation was simply a convex fold plunging into the earth.

Given plate tectonic theory, with its mechanisms of crustal movement and subduction, the Olympics are now seen as an ancient chain of submarine volcanic peaks that rested on sea floor sediments. As the ocean floor moved toward the continent, the sediments and the basalts perched upon them formed a wedge caught between crust subducting beneath the continent and the continental plate margin. Compressed between the colliding plates, the material has fractured into large zones along fault lines and undergone tremendous deformation within smaller rock units. Some theorists believe that the horseshoe shape of the Crescent basalt formation is the result of its being form-fitted against the ancient edge of the continent.

Intense erosion has carved the peaks of the Olympics we see today. Glacial erosion has left its bite-marks in the form of cirque basins and steepened peaks of once-higher mountains. Valley systems of the western slopes show evidence of alpine glaciers reaching far into the lowlands, where they deposited large glacial moraines, like the one that formed the basin of Quinault Lake. Flooded with precipitation from the nearby Pacific, Olympic rivers continue deepening the valleys, carrying the stuff of the mountains back to the ocean.

Western Olympics, with the exception of Olympus itself, are the lower peaks of the range, reflecting their softer rock. Mt. Tom, a western spur of the Mt. Olympus massif, stands 7,048 feet high. Few other peaks west of Olympus are higher than 5,000 feet.

East of Olympus, the range as a whole consists of higher and steeper country. Crescent formation basalts—more erosion-resistant than the marine shales and sand-

Facing page: Mt. Olympus (background, 7,965'), dominates the mountain landscape of the western Olympics. The Bailey Range (foreground) forms an important divide between the moist western part of the Olympics and the "rainshadow" of the east. Above: The Graywolf Needles of Crescent Formation basalts, the remnants of an upended undersea volcano chain that forms a semicircle enclosing most of the Olympic Mountains. In the distance, Mt. Baker and Mt. Shuksan. PAT O'HARA PHOTOS

stones—contribute some of the more dramatic relief. Mount Constance (7,743') and the twin-summited Brothers (6,866'), top the Olympic skyline as viewed from Seattle. Both are composed entirely of the sea-floor volcanics. The Graywolf Needles, also formed of up-ended basalt beds, form a rampart of spires above the high, dry ridges that characterize the Olympics' northeast corner.

Another elaborate complex of peaks and glaciers is located in the vicinity of Mt. Anderson, in the headwaters of the East Fork of the Quinault River. Located just inside the southern rim of the basalt horseshoe, Mt. Anderson (7,321') consists of deeply folded sandstones. Glacial activity on the flanks of Anderson reveals a sequence of moraines formed quite recently as the Anderson glacier has retreated up its bed. In its present state, the Anderson glacier has the disheveled look of an aging recluse, hunkering into a soft armchair.

Recently deglaciated landscapes are scattered throughout the Olympics. These raw, hummocky basins reveal the various stages of succession between occupations of cold ice and verdant forest. Lower portions of Seven Lakes Basin have been partially reclaimed by "upwardly mobile" forests. Dotted with lakes (actually there are eight), the area is heavily visited by backpackers. Cam-

Above: Mt. Anderson (7,321'). Facing page: Mt. Bretherton and Upper Lena Lake, in the Olympics' southeast corner. PAT O'HARA PHOTOS

eron Basin and Lost Pass, in the northeast part of Olympic National Park, are also vivid examples of landscapes recently unburdened of glacial ice.

Throughout the eastern Olympics, lightning strikes and wildfire have contributed to the mosaic of plant communities. Dryness owing to the "rain-shadow effect" both aids and hinders the spread of wildfire—high forests are usually tinder-dry much of the summer, but patchy in composition, creating elaborate natural fire-breaks of intervening canyons and rock outcrops. Fire is a significant force in shaping the natural order here. Douglas fir forests and elk both are the beneficiaries of the cycle of fire induced by climatic regimes.

The effect created by the Olympics as a rain-barrier is startling. The mountainous divide creates a border between areas that receive the highest and lowest annual rainfall recorded in western Washington. Broad glacier valleys on the western slope are home to temperate rain forest communities rare in the northern hemisphere. Glacier-laid soils, volume of precipitation and proximity to fog belts of the ocean have given rise to some of the most productive temperate forests known. Meanwhile, across the divide created by the Olympics, areas of the San Juan Islands and coastal plains northeast of the mountains often receive less than 16 inches of precipitation annually—making this region the driest along the Pacific Coast of the U.S. north of San Diego County, California.

Life zones represented in the Olympics include the Lowland Humid Transition, the Montane, the Subalpine and the Alpine. Western hemlock forests dominate the lowland (sea-level to approximately 2,500 feet of elevation), often mixed with western red cedar. Sitka spruce dominates the lowland forest within the moist belt near the coast. Douglas fir is found in the lowlands as well, primarily in areas where it has been planted extensively for silvicultural purposes and in dry areas with gravelly, excessively-drained soils. Deciduous forests are found in river corridors and in cutover areas not replanted with conifers. Red alder, bigleaf maple, Pacific dogwood, black cottonwood and a host of willows are the most commonly found broadleaf species.

Montane forests (approximately 2,500' to 4,000' of elevation) also contain significant stands of western hemlock, although the tapestry is made richer by the addition of Pacific silver fir on the moist western slopes and by the substitution of Douglas fir on drier eastern slopes. Other montane conifers include Engelmann spruce in a few isolated patches of the northeastern Olympics and Pacific yew on rocky slopes. Western white pine is sprinkled through the dry-side forests—as elsewhere through its western North America range, it suffers from white pine blister-rust, a fungal parasite lethal to the tree.

Other montane plants include blueberry, sword and bracken fern, and devil's club, the bane of the bushwhacker. Avalanche tracks often penetrate deep into the valleys and form a unique plant community composed of

Above: Roosevelt elk in Olympic National Park. TOM & PAT LEESON

Right: Mildred Lakes and reflections. PAT O'HARA

lithe trees like slide alder and fleshy herbs like cow parsnip. Both plants are able, through different mechanisms, to survive the unique disturbance of living in lanes frequented by thunderous slides that make matchsticks of stiffer trees but which have little effect on limber, prostrate trunks or overwintering roots that survive year after year underground.

The Olympic subalpine zone (approximately 4,000' to 5,000') is particularly noted for lush meadows arrayed with vivid splashes of wildflowers. Drier meadows support beargrass, lupine, American bistort and many other species. Wet meadows hold rein orchids, Jeffrey's shooting star and elephant-head pedicularis. Subalpine rockeries bloom with wild onions, smooth Douglasia, stonecrop and a wide variety of daisies and asters.

Subalpine forests are dominated by subalpine fir and mountain hemlock in moister regions; subalpine fir and lodgepole pine in drier regions. Whitebark pine makes its appearance in a few places along the high ridges of the northeast. Yellow cedar is found throughout the Olympic subalpine, often assuming stunted forms in response to climatic brutality.

The subalpine faunal assemblage is similar to those of other Washington ranges with several notable exceptions. Several prominent animals found in adjacent mountain ranges are missing in the Olympics. Examples include pika, ptarmigan, bighorn sheep and mountain goat. Mountain goats were introduced in the 1920s to enhance hunting opportunity, and are now present in local concentrations high enough that they appear to cause significant alteration to fragile plant communities. Certain plants appear to be disrupted by wallowing, trampling and feeding activities where the animals gather in large numbers. Active research and a variety of management measures have been taken to better understand the goats and their impacts. Endemic mammals include the Olympic marmot, Olympic chipmunk and Olympic snowmole.

Above the tree line, ridgelines undulate and steepen. The land itself dominates the eye. Distantly, the curve of earth and the shimmer of sun on the ocean become visible. Without a soft cloak of living things, the land breaks into eroded summits and the veins of dissected valleys. Here especially, is raw, elemental landscape, where ocean and continent are vividly one, united in one sweeping glance.

Left: Marymere Falls. Above: Columbia lily. Below: Pacific bleeding hearts and evergreen violets. PAT O'HARA PHOTOS

CHAPTER EIGHT

THE YOUNG VOLCANICS

Pink fireweed regrowth, Mt. St. Helens blast area, 1984. TOM & PAT LEESON

Mt. Rainier. PAT O'HARA

The tent shook violently. My thin sleep was pierced again by arrows of waking that were plaguing this particular night. "Why," I wondered, "can't I just fall asleep and stay that way until I am supposed to wake up and climb this mountain." My inner voice was being urgent. I would need the sleep for the slog. We were off-route, 1,000 feet below and east of Dog's Head on a pre-eruptive Mt. St. Helens and the wind was now blowing very hard. In white-out conditions that afternoon we had left the timberline parking lot, trudged across the Plains of Abraham and nearly succeeded in missing the invisible mountain entirely. Sleeplessness was compounded by a number of things. I was nervous about my first (and only) "big volcano" climb, we had retired at 6 p.m., and I was sure that the seams of the tent were about to unravel with each fresh gust.

When I began to relax the dream returned. The world was white. Figure and ground were blended by opaque light. I was afoot, in snow, and standing. I was alone. I heard a rush of wings and out of the white a raven flew. The bird grew blacker as it approached me—fuzzy at first, then sharp. Other than myself, only the raven was visible. It passed quickly, just over my head and a few feet away, uttering a chesty croak as it flew by. Its outline became a smudge and it vanished—as quickly as it came. Sometime shortly afterward, my partner awakened me.

"Summit time."

At the beginning of the world, everything was white except Raven. He was flying past the mountain...

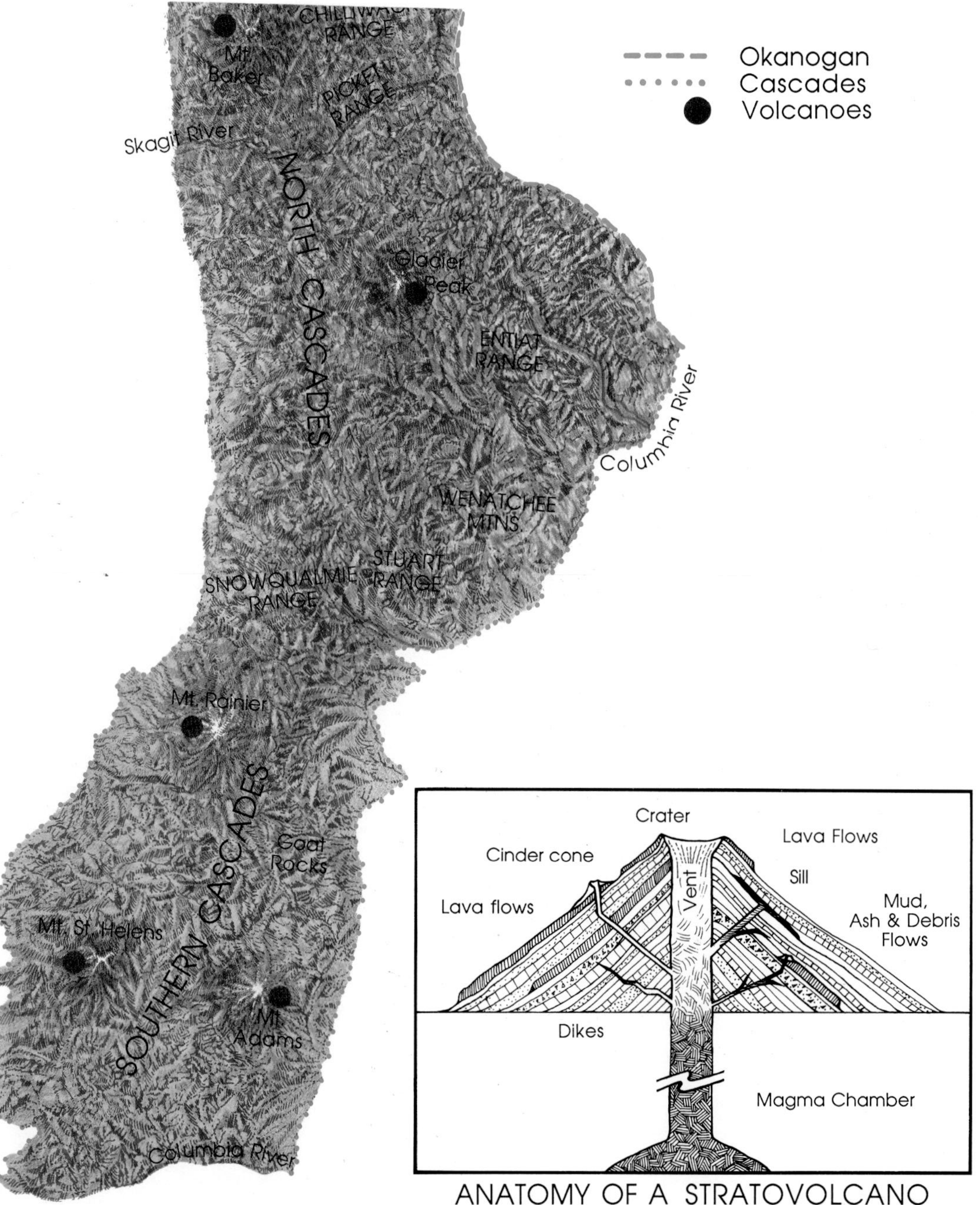

ANATOMY OF A STRATOVOLCANO

Washington's volcanoes have to be considered the state's pre-eminent landforms. They billow out of the horizon like sentient beings. When the seemingly ever-present cloudiness of western Washington parts for Rainier to make a transitive appearance, "a day" becomes "a Day." Haloed by lenticular clouds during a winter arctic high pressure system, any of the big mountains becomes a presence rather than simply a feature of the land.

Indeed, humans have always held the volcanoes in awe. Prehistoric soap operas were based on the torrid love triangles and other intrigues in the lives of the Cascade volcanoes. Accounts of prehistoric eruptions and mud-

flows became the weft of an oral tapestry, the cloth of history that native northwesterners wrapped around their tribes and their origins. In these mountains the sublime forces of imagination and reality combine. These are the faces that bring God to mind, regardless of one's creed. The forces that give rise to the Cascade volcanoes are not mysterious. But their suddenness and terrible intensity inspire our awe.

In the historical era, eruptions all over the globe have captured the attention of astute observers. A credible body of explanations had been devised before Washington State was even settled. Terminology derived from Greek, Latin, even Polynesian, has been used to describe the products and events that shape the young Cascades. In many senses, what happens here is no different than what has happened many other places, when mountains have been formed, or destroyed, by volcanic processes.

Nevertheless, Washington's volcanic peaks have made their own contribution to the worldwide understanding of the explosive processes that build these giants. Mechanisms of subduction are well focused here. Evidence of the effects of vast mudflows and rockfalls, triggered by deep earthquakes, have been studied on the Washington peaks. Summit cone-building episodes, the distribution of ash, and many other subjects are well illustrated in the active volcanic chain of Washington state. And with the sequence of events that preceded and followed the St. Helens eruption of May 18, 1980, the scientific literature of these mountains burgeoned.

If we view the gradual building of the Cascade Range over time, with the metaphor of masonry construction, we can envision the addition of the big volcanoes—Baker, Glacier Peak, Rainier, Adams and St. Helens—as the overnight blossoming of tents on a foundation of bricks. By comparison, the mountains we see towering above the rest of the range are just as temporary. The once-symmetrical cone of St. Helens makes the case well. Here today, gone tomorrow.

Washington's Quaternary volcanoes (so-called because they have been formed within the Quaternary period—the million years or so that coincide with the presence of humans on the planet) are the most active in the 48 connected United States. Except for Mt. Lassen, at the southern end of the Cascade chain, no others have breathed more than brief sighs since adjacent regions have been settled. A minor explosive eruption occurred on Mt. Rainier sometime around 1850. Mt. Baker had minor explosive eruptions in 1843, 1854, 1858, 1859 and 1870. Steam emissions increased in 1975 and continue through the present. Mt. Adams remains quiescent except for minor gas and steam emissions. Glacier Peak appears to have been still for most of the last 10,000 years. Mt. St. Helens has demonstrated the greatest activity, as well as the fact that the forces of subduction that drive Cascade volcanism are working now, somewhere beneath us.

The Cascade volcanoes belong to a category of volcanic features known as composite or stratovolcanoes. Stratovolcanoes, as the name implies, are made up of many layers of lava interleaved with mudflow and ash debris. Unlike cinder cones, which are composed mostly of uniform ash material, and shield volcanoes, which are broad, gently sloping lava structures, stratovolcanoes are complex heaps of material with varying rates of erosion and structural integrity. Remnants of earlier cones or vent systems are often exposed in the eroding flanks of Cascade volcanoes. Surrounding valleys show signs of past mudflows or hot ash avalanches.

Washington's Quaternary volcanoes are chronologically and structurally more closely related to each other than to the formations upon which they rest. All are driven by the same force—the subduction of the Juan de Fuca plate beneath the margin of the North American plate—and all produce similar rock types.

While most rocks in the Cascades vary in age from between 570 and 50 million years, the stratovolcanoes we know today appear to be considerably less than 100,000 years old. Evidence suggests that Mt. Rainier attained its maximum size about 75,000 years ago and that Mt. St. Helens has evolved mostly within the last 2,000 years. Numerous episodes of volcanism preceded the construction of the young peaks, including the construction of shield volcanoes in some areas of the Western Cascades as recently as 2 million years ago, shortly after the Cascade Range began its uplift.

Mt. Baker

Mt. Baker was named for Third Lieutenant Joseph Baker, an officer and cartographer under Vancouver, who saw the mountain in April 1792, as Vancouver's expedition sailed east into the Strait of Juan de Fuca. It ranks fourth in height of the Washington peaks, at 10,778 feet of elevation. The mountain is cloaked by glaciers that radiate away from its several summits, the largest being the Coleman and Sherman glaciers. Glaciers form the headwaters of the major drainage systems including the Nooksack River on the north and west, and the Baker River, a tributary of the Skagit, on the south and east.

Mt. Baker attracted attention in 1975, when steam eruptions were seen coming from the Sherman Crater, south of the summit dome. Thermal activity continues; however, no other eruptive activity has been noted. Baker's present crater marks the third in a series of identifiable activity centers on the mountain. The first, the Black Buttes, about two miles southwest of the present summit, is thought to be approximately 400,000 years

Facing page: Mt. Baker and Coleman Pinnacle.
Above: Coleman Glacier and Headwall, Mt. Baker. PAT O'HARA PHOTOS

Mt. Baker's First Ascent

Koma Kulshan, a broad, snowy monarch, gleams over the northern Sound on a winter day clear as a whip-crack. Vancouver named it for an Englishman on a spring day, unaware that two years earlier, the Spaniard Quimper (or one of his officers) had named it Gran Montaña de Carmelo.

By 1868, the mountain was clearly known as Mt. Baker, ensconced on all the maps as one of the Cascades' remotest volcanoes, unvisited and unclimbed. At this time the major heights of Europe had felt the pricks of nailed boots and alpenstocks and the truly adventurous were seeking the summits of other continents. So it was that Edmund T. Coleman, Englishman, artist, and charter member of the Alpine Club, resolved to "leave the beaten paths of the European ice-fields for the unexplored heights of the West."

Coleman took up residence in Victoria, painted local scenes, secured a post as a librarian and began preparations for an ascent of Mt. Baker, visible from the prominence of Cedar Hill near town. Three attempts were eventually made, one was successful. In a time when sophisticated mountain travelers spent as much time during the approach calling on distinguished local residents as hacking through underbrush, Coleman's progress was understandably slow. After weathering the society circuit of blooming towns of Sehome and Whatcom (later to fuse as Bellingham), Coleman entered the wilderness, poling up the swollen Nooksack River in Indian canoes and hiking "over fallen trees, under old logs, down steep ravines, over high rough rocks, and through close-set jungle."

By and by the party, consisting of Coleman and locals David Ogilvie, Thomas Stratton and John Tennant, emerged from the dank lowlands into the subalpine world, where Coleman noted plants that "were all good illustrations of Darwin's theory of natural selection, having short thick stems to enable them to withstand the storms of their exposed situation." Coleman also revealed a reverent streak:

Edmund T. Coleman's 1868 first ascent of Mt. Baker was described in detail in an article, "Mountaineering on the Pacific," in Harpers New Monthly Magazine. *Coleman's own illustrations are entitled (above) "Extinct crater showing Mount Grant, the main peak" and (right) "Ascending the rapids."*

Far left: "Putting through"; near left: "Grant's Peak, the summit."

"It was Sunday morning, and the stillness of the scenery made us vividly realize its holy associations.... We were in a temple not made with hands. There was no need of Sabbath bell to sound the call to worship. The sublimity of the scene lifted us above all worldly considerations, all thoughts of self, and evoked involuntary exclamations of praise."

Coleman and party succeeded in planting the American flag atop Mt. Baker after overcoming all manner of alpine hazards. The group also took the opportunity to view the active crater of the volcano; Stratton was so overcome by the odor of sulphur that he reportedly vomited.

Coleman's mixture of sociability, Continental climbing mannerisms, and artistic and literary temperament contributed an element previously lacking in northwest mountaineering. His was the mission of the amateur, not the empire builder or savant. Alpinism, the recreational pursuit of mountaintops—European-style—had immigrated to Washington's mountains.

"Studio in the mountains."

American Border Peak. PAT O'HARA

old. The Black Buttes are now heavily eroded as the Thunder and Deming glaciers have gnawed into the ridge, forming impressive cirque basins. The present summit, known as Grant Peak, was the second scene of volcanic activity and is thought to be older than the most recent glacial epoch (approximately 10,000 years ago) because of the presence of deeply eroded cirques on the north wall of the peak. The Coleman and Roosevelt glaciers have bitten deeply into the mountain, creating the Coleman Headwall and spur ridges known as the North Ridge, Cockscomb and the Roman Nose.

Volcanic material associated with Mt. Baker sits astride a series of very old rock, marine sandstones formed long before they were attached to the continent. Just east of the mountain is the Shuksan Thrust Fault, a deep boundary between formations of heavily metamorphosed submarine basalts (greenschists) and underlying sediments of the Chilliwack Group. Chilliwack Group sediments are thought to be somewhere between 200 and 300 million years of age; Shuksan Suite greenschists, 100 to 150 million years old. Baker's pediment is probably older than that of other Washington Cascade volcanoes.

The geologic complexity of the region is largely responsible for its appeal to mountaineers—the Mt. Baker vicinity holds some of Washington's most challenging ascents. While Baker itself is quite straightforward in its simpler routes (the Coleman-Deming Glacier route receives the most travel), weather on the mountain is extremely variable and numerous more difficult routes dot the mountainside. Baker also holds a rich cultural heritage in its long and colorful history of ascents, attempts and tragedies.

Glacier Peak

Glacier Peak is the least seen of the Washington volcanoes, tucked deep in the heart of the range and well beyond the reach of any roads. Glacier is the fifth highest peak in Washington, its summit reaching 10,541 feet above sea level. Its name, bestowed by early surveyors, may not seem particularly evocative, but is especially accurate in a descriptive sense. Glacier sits aloof and cool, surrounded by walls of adjacent peaks and moats of deeply incised river valleys. Perhaps more than any other of the Quaternary volcanoes, Glacier suggests wilderness and inaccessibility.

Glacier's geologic history presents a few new twists in the general outline of youth, fury and erosion seen in the other Washington volcanoes. The mountain formed as a growing vent along a pre-existing ridge composed of North Cascades micro-continent gneisses. Volcanic rock in the vicinity reveals volcanic activity that pre-dates the "modern" activity by many millions of years. Pinkish rhyolites, lava of composition similar to granite, spilled over the region, filling valleys which later eroded away, leaving the lava perched atop the new ridges. After a long period of quiet, forces of subduction created new volcanic activity in the area, activity that has occurred mostly in the fairly recent past. This time, andesite was produced, liquid and flowing at first, followed by eruptions of much blockier, sluggish andesite at later times. The later flows created a pluglike dome on the mountain now called Disappointment Peak. Other explosive eruptions created enormous debris avalanches that partially filled the Suiattle River Valley with a large debris fan.

Sometime about 12,000 years ago, the mountain exploded with great fury, sending ash and airborne

Left: Glacier Peak and Image Lake. Above: Glaciers forming on the Cascade Crest near Glacier Peak scooped out broad, U-shaped valleys, including the Napeequa Valley, seen here. PAT O'HARA PHOTOS

Loving Mountains to Death

Left to right: The popularity of major routes on Mt. Rainier has contributed significantly to ecological damage in the alpine environment. Solar-assisted vault privies concentrate human waste: evaporation lessens its weight for airlift down the mountain. Tent City at Camp Muir, 10,000'. GEORGE WUERTHNER PHOTOS

Mt. Rainier looms above the horizon, a vast mound of snowfields, broken rock walls and cataracts of flowing ice. Born in volcanic fury, a magnet to violent weather and dwarfing everything of human scale, the mountain suggests invulnerability—at times, hostility—toward human beings. It is perhaps this impression that makes poignant our desire to climb to Rainier's summit, to answer its challenge, to "conquer" the snowy dome, 14,410 feet above sea level.

The challenge of climbing Rainier is taken up by about 7,500 climbers annually. Weather usually determines success or failure—only 56 to 61 percent of summit attempts result in success. The two most popular routes, the Muir Corridor and the Emmons Glacier, bear most of the traffic, and along both routes, humans have extracted a toll from the mountain and its fragile alpine ecosystems.

On the upper slopes of Rainier, human solid waste has created conditions that seriously compromise the safe drinking of melted snow-water as well as the aesthetics of the mountain's sparkling firn. Bacterial growth that at lower elevations would aid in the decomposition of fecal material is absent due to low temperature and high exposure to solar radiation. Fecal material literally becomes part of the snowpack, accumulating year after year along most highly traveled routes. That which is removed from high-country privies amounts to an estimated 12,000 pounds every year.

Fragile "fellfields," stone fields that harbor delicate plant communities, have been destroyed by climbing parties clearing the cobbled ground for tent platforms and using the stones to construct windbreaks for tents and stoves. Forty-two species of alpine plants utilize the fellfield habitat, 20 of which do not occur below 7,000 feet of elevation. Plants uniquely adapted to the harsh living conditions have fallen victim to transient human visitors who have disrupted the fragile balance of microclimates

created in the shelter of the stones in their natural configuration. Elsewhere in the alpine zone, heather communities, thought to be hundreds of years old, suffer from the creation of braided footpaths as hikers and climbers seek to avoid trench-like pathways trampled in the snow along popular routes.

High-country campsites like Camp Muir and Camp Shurman, overnight stopovers for the majority of summit attempts, have become garbage collection points, latrines stuffed with non-organic litter deposited by crowds of summit-bound climbers.

In an effort to maintain the ecological and aesthetic integrity of the alpine zone, the National Park Service has instituted a number of regulations and management techniques. Quotas were established in 1973, based on the carrying capacity of given areas. Sanitary facilities were developed, including a solar-assisted evaporation privy at Camp Muir and privacy screens installed at Ingraham Flats and Emmons Flats to aid in concentrating human waste in areas where it can conveniently be collected and removed from the mountain. The Park Service even provides individual "human waste" bags in the ultimate expression of the philosophy of "Pack It Out."

In addition, studies were undertaken to ascertain the sensitivity of alpine plant communities to human disturbance; regulations have been adopted to protect the fell-fields and heather communities.

The challenge that pits human strength and ingenuity against nature's elements is fundamental to mountaineering, indeed to survival itself in truly wild environments. Yet the distinction is narrowly drawn between triumph over and contempt of forces that outscale humanness so grandly. Rainier hosts such forces; it is our intent that must be scrutinized. Is despoliation of a rare fragment of nature an inevitable result of our desire to conquer her?

Revegetation of braided trails in the subalpine zone has helped heal scars of human impact—damage to the alpine zone, higher on the mountain, may not be so easy to repair.
GEORGE WUERTHNER PHOTOS

Mount Rainier from the north. The imposing shadow of the 4,000' Mt. Willis Wall reveals the erosive power of the Carbon Glacier. Little Tahoma, on the left skyline, is Washington's third highest peak (11,117').
PAT O'HARA

debris well into Saskatchewan. The cataclysm left its ash legacy over much of the regions north and east of the peak, but unlike another well known ash-producing eruption, that of Mt. Mazama 6,600 years ago, the mountain's summit did not collapse. Glacier became quiet following its major blowout of 12,000 years ago. Subsequent volcanic activity has occurred in the form of nearby cinder-cone eruptions—short-lived and not terribly damaging—and some thermal spring activity around the mountain's base.

As evidenced in its name, Glacier Peak lies buried beneath great masses of ice—12 square miles of it, including the Suiattle and White Chuck glaciers on spur flanks. Names like Chocolate, Scimitar, Dusty, Cool, Ermine, Guardian, and Vista give the mountain the evocative character that the peak's own name lacks. The ice tongues gouge at the mountain, forming great scarp shoulders on the north and west. The Suiattle River sweeps around the mountain in a semicircle from southeast to northwest gathering up the runoff from a dozen glaciers, carrying the silt to faraway Puget Sound.

Mt. Rainier

Mt. Rainier has greater affinity to sky than to land. As though it were a permanent jumble of cumulus, billowing and bright, The Mountain hangs where no land should be, miles above the lowland plain. Rainier so dominates the Washington skyline that on a clear day you can orient yourself quickly, whether amid the prickly summits of the North Cascades or the jumbled canyons of downtown Seattle.

The mountain's name generated intense controversy until the 1920s. Patriotic Americans long favored something more homegrown than the name of a British naval officer with a reputation of capturing American vessels during the Revolutionary War. Tacomans too felt that the mountain deserved the name "Tahoma," or "Tacoma," the name originally bestowed upon it—one that reflected favorably on their ambitious city.

At 14,410', Mt. Rainier stands just a shade beneath California's Mt. Whitney as the highest point in the lower 48 states. While Whitney's "achievement" is owed to the height of the upthrust Sierra Nevada around it, Rainier can claim its own glory—it clears the surrounding peaks by nearly 8,000'. And ironically, Washington's third highest peak, Little Tahoma (11,117'), is lost entirely when it falls into the afternoon shade of Rainier.

Rainier's geologic history is well understood. Traces of basement rock are visible in surrounding lowlands that suggest a fairly complete chronology of events leading to the building of the mountain we know today. About 40 to 50 million years ago, the region now occupied by the western Cascades was a low coastal plain, harboring rich forests, bogs and slowly rising and falling shoreline. Rich deposits of coal in the Black Diamond District attest to the accumulation of decaying organic material that took place over tens of millions of years. Early volcanic activity accompanied the jostlings of uplift as tectonic forces began altering the continental margin. Lava flows,

represented in the Ohanapecosh, Stevens Ridge and Fife's Peak formations, spread over the land and injections of granodiorite formed the Tatoosh Pluton. All of these form the foundation upon which the present volcano sits.

The Cascades continued their uplift, warping and folding and eroding steadily as the range emerged and began creating a barrier that captured onshore wind currents and squeezed out precipitation through cooling and condensation.

Although the date is not recorded in the rocks with certainty, the volcano was born sometime between 2 million and 25,000 years ago. Throughout its building stage, glaciers formed, carving what mountain there was, melting and collapsing in mud-ice torrents when the mountain stirred.

The cycle of eruption, lava and ash deposition, glacial erosion and deposition, returning to eruption, has repeated itself countless times during the period in which Rainier has grown from a cinder cone to the volcanic monarch it is. Lava, ash, mud and glacial rubble form a jumbled matrix throughout the mountain. Pumice deposits, representing events when molten, foaming rock ash were blown out of the mountain, are visible in the eastern portions of Mt. Rainier National Park. These were formed during eruptions that have occurred since the Ice Age. Other evidence of such activity is found in mud flows that followed river valleys at the mountain's foot and rockslides triggered, in part, by seismic activity within the mountain.

Sometime approximately 5,800 years ago, Rainier's summit, then about 16,000 feet above sea level, collapsed, resulting in a huge mudflow covering nearly 125 square miles of lowland that is now heavily populated. Named the Osceola Mudflow, it is the largest known on earth. Eruptions continued into the present era. Historic eruptions have been slight, yet the potential exists that, at

Left: Eruptions in the last several thousand years have left parts of the Mt. Rainier region covered with pumice fragments.
Center and above: Mt. Rainier has many faces. Stevens Canyon shows its fall colors and stately conifers rise out of vine maple in the Grove of the Patriarchs, Mt. Rainier National Park. PAT O'HARA PHOTOS

Above: Winter enfolds the Tatoosh Range, near Mt. Rainier.
Facing page: Mt. Adams (12,276'), Washington's second highest peak.
PAT O'HARA PHOTOS

any time, ash, mud, lava and general chaos will issue from the mountain.

Such is the dynamic life of a volcano. Yet, for its sheer power and potential destructiveness, Rainier yields a softer presence. On its lower slopes, lilies, lupines and gentians spread over the gentle slopes like debris fans of past avalanches. Lake-studded high country rings the mountain. Below the subalpine zone, verdant worlds of lowland and montane forests anchor the mountain's supernal visage to the places of people, places that we best understand and that afford relative comfort. Its familiar forms of life connect Rainier to the rest of the world.

Mt. Adams

Mt. Adams was first viewed by whites when Captain William Clark of the Lewis and Clark Expedition climbed a basalt cliff overlooking what were once the Umatilla Rapids of the Columbia River. He mistook it for Mt. St. Helens, known then from Vancouver's journals (Elliott Coues, editor of the 1893 edition of Lewis' and Clark's journals, believed Clark was accurate in his sighting of St. Helens). For the bone-weary expedition the mountain—whatever it was—was a welcome sight. The "Snowy Range," promised to lie near the Pacific, was close.

Adams was known by other names to Indians. Variously "Klickitat" or "Pahto," the mountain was one of a trio of peaks that figured prominently in a love-battle chronicled by legend as the war between rival mountains from opposite sides of the river (Wyeast or Mt. Hood and Klickitat or Mt. Adams) for the hand of a lovely maiden, Loo-wit (Mt. St. Helens).

The name we know is a relic of a patriotic scheme to memorialize early U.S. presidents by naming major Cascade peaks after them. Only Thomas Jefferson and John Adams bear such distinction—Adams actually by error when the name intended for Mt. St. Helens was misplaced on the map. As it turned out, there was a mountain where the name was placed after all. It was Pahto or Klickitat or whatever. It's now called Adams.

Adams is Washington's second highest peak, reaching to 12,276 feet above sea level. Massive from every perspective, and relatively isolated, it is noticed but largely unknown to most Washingtonians. The peak is actually a complex series of cones that seem to prop one another up, patterned as an ovoid lump along a north-south axis. One striking pattern is noticeable on Adams—that its southwest-facing slope is rather smooth and its other faces are deeply cut into headwalls, cleavers and broken ridges. The presence of aggressive glaciation only partly accounts for this. It is believed that in its latest eruptive stages, cinders and other pyroclastic material have swept over the southwest slope building a smooth surface. Adams' several peaks each are thought to represent the products of different active events.

Other distinctive volcanic features of Mt. Adams include satellite cinder cones at the foot of the mountain—side channels off the vent system within the mountain that have had brief lives sometime in the not-too-distant past. Sulphur deposits near the summit are also unusual among the Cascade volcanoes. Sulphur gasses issuing through the relict vents condense on the loose cinder debris. Mining claims were staked in 1929 and sulphur extracted for many years.

REJUVENATION ON MT. ST. HELENS

Mt. St. Helens, squat and gaping. The faded sky-blue of dozens of color calendars replaced instead by a neutral gray as familiar as a stack of newspapers. And news it was. A day indelible in the memory of each Washingtonian. Where were you when the mountain blew?

Some were too close. Geologists, family campers, an irascible Harry Truman and others perished when the mountainside collapsed, uncorking earth's inner fury. Forests died on nearly 151,000 productive acres. Trout streams boiled. Lakes, once gems in a forested setting, were choked with debris—animal, vegetable and mineral—cooking from the heat of the blast. Wildlife losses were staggering: 1,500 elk, 5,000 blacktailed deer, 15 mountain goats (the entire Mt. Margaret population) as well as countless other small mammals, birds, amphibians and other animals. The land was a ruin. Tree-stems flattened in the blast pointed in the direction whence death had come. The mountain crater smoldered, bare, culpable.

Yet living continued. Patches where volcanic ash debris was thin sprouted living plants, rooted in soil. Erosion carried away large quantities of the unstable debris mantle, revealing buried soil and plants already in sprout when the eruption occurred. Ground shielded from direct heat and force of the blast by lingering snowdrifts yielded its precious living inhabitants. Fireweed, lupine, huckleberries and tree seedlings grew rapidly. Death was not uniform in the blast swath. Sheltered places held scattered remnants of living things, which bloomed into life and burst into new territory. For all the St. Helens eruption of May 18, 1980, taught scientists of destruction, it also taught of renewal, of the resilience of living things after catastrophe.

Although evidence of past volcanic fury is found throughout the world, the St. Helens eruption afforded scientific specialists of many disciplines a rare opportunity to study the return of life to a barren landscape, one wiped clean of signs of life in a few moments of volcanic rage.

Foresters and fisheries biologists evaluated the effects of the eruption on resources of obvious economic importance. Botanists and zoologists found within the devastated area a wealth of information about mechanisms of survival, seed dispersal, competition and behavioral adaptation. Each link in the chain of living things was reforged, the vacuum that nature abhors was filled. Organisms found appropriate niches, from algae growing in mineral-rich muck, to ants foraging on minute fungus patches, to elk, regrouping their herds and seeking the forage of isolated patches of vegetation that began emerging as the eruption receded into the past.

One of the most startling responses to the calamity was that of the Toutle River salmon run. Returning up the Columbia and Cowlitz rivers, the salmon sensed the change in their natal stream and returned downstream to the

Facing page: Mt. St. Helens on May 18, 1980 © GARY BRAASCH *and from the air in 1983.* PAT O'HARA
Above: Steam plume from the crater dome, high inside the crater, Mt. St. Helens, 1984. JEFF GNASS

Left to right: Steam rises from St. Helens' crater. Scattered debris recalls the forces that gave the mountain and the land around it a new face.
The growing lava dome inside the crater has given geologists the opportunity to see a new mountain in the making.
The Toutle River carves deeply into a "lahar," a plateau of volcanic debris.
Finality has no place among the cycles that make and change mountains. The transformation characterized as destruction at St. Helens continues today as the mountain and the life-forms it hosts undergo rebirth. PHOTOS © GARY BRAASCH

Facing page: Mt. St. Helens in 1980, the view to Mt. Adams from Spirit Lake. © GARY BRAASCH

Columbia. Finding the next river hospitable, they made their spawning run on the Kalama—adopting that river as their "new" ancestral stream.

The ability of plants and animals to survive and to recolonize was put to the test. Some plant communities, surviving the blast itself, withered under the drought that accompanied exposure to the summer sun. Fishes and amphibians, protected in chilly lakes under the late-spring snow cover during the eruption, died later as aquatic food sources failed. Colonizers, the so-called "pioneers" of succession, including red alder, lupine, thistle, vetch and blackberries invaded disturbed areas aggressively. Red alder, lupine and vetch, all capable of fixing atmospheric nitrogen in the soil, enrich the new soils with critical nitrogen as well as their own decaying roots, leaves and stems as they eventually die.

Such a vivid scene of contrast, of dramatic differences between primal forces of earth and the tender forces of life, are readily visible at Mt. St. Helens. Lost in the immediate drama, however, is the reality that such events have frequently punctuated the stillness of the coevolution of organisms with landscape. Signs throughout the pre-eruptive Mt. St. Helens region attested to other catastrophes. Douglas fir tree rings revealed similar eruptions in 1480 and 1800, when the steady growth of the tree was checked by a decade of very slow growth.

Throughout the volcanic Cascades, the signs of such give and take are found. Centuries of the orderly elaboration of living systems are erased in the holocaust of a moment. The moment passes and is compressed into a thin ash layer in the soil or the genetic make-up of a population of survivors. Faint thumbprints of change, vague remembrances etched in life itself, are all that remain of Vulcan's heavy hand. A re-assortment takes place and that assortment struggles to become the new ecologic order. It will succeed until the mountain itself finds new life. Then it will succumb to the forces and spring into another inevitable surge of renewal.

As a way of preserving the process of renewal at Mt. St. Helens, Congress established the Mount St. Helens National Volcanic Monument in 1982. The legislation mandated the U.S. Forest Service to administer 110,000 acres for public recreation, education and research. Campgrounds, trails and interpretive centers have been built, enabling visitors to witness, firsthand, the return of life to the St. Helens landscape.

WASHINGTON'S 50 TALLEST PEAKS

Rank and Name	Elev. (ft.)	First Ascent	Region
1. Mt. Rainier	14,410	1870	Cascade volcano
2. Mt. Adams	12,276	1854	Cascade volcano
3. Little Tahoma	11,117	1895	Cascade volcano
4. Mt. Baker	10,778	1868	Cascade volcano
5. Glacier Peak	10,541	1898	Cascade volcano
6. Disappointment Peak (Glacier Peak)	9,755	unkn	Cascade volcano
7. Bonanza Peak	9,511	1937	North Cascades
8. Colfax Peak (Mt. Baker)	9,443	1921	Cascade volcano
9. Mt. Stuart	9,415	1873	South Cascades
10. Sitkum Spire	9,355	1961	North Cascades
11. Mt. Fernow	9,249	1932	North Cascades
12. Mt. Goode	9,200+	1936	North Cascades
13. Mt. Shuksan	9,127	1906	North Cascades
14. Lincoln Peak	9,096	1956	North Cascades
15. Mt. Logan	9,087	1926	North Cascades
16. Mt. Maude	9,082	1932	North Cascades
17. Mt. Buckner	9,080	1901	North Cascades
18. Seven-Fingered Jack	9,077	1932	North Cascades
19. Jack Mountain	9,060	1904	North Cascades
20. Mesahchie Peak	8,975	1966	North Cascades
21. Black Peak	8,970	1926	North Cascades
22. Copper Peak	8,966	1937	North Cascades
23. Mt. Redoubt	8,956	1930	North Cascades
24. North Gardner	8,956	1898	North Cascades
25. Dome Peak	8,920+	1936	North Cascades
26. Gardner Mountain	8,897	1898	North Cascades
27. Boston Peak	8,894	1938	North Cascades
28. Mt. Spickard	8,879	1904	North Cascades
29. Silver Star Mt.	8,876	1926	North Cascades
30. Eldorado Peak	8,868	1933	North Cascades
31. K's Spire	8,849	1951	South Cascades
32. Dragontail Peak	8,840	1937	South Cascades
33. Peak 8824	8,824	1961	North Cascades
34. Forbidden Peak	8,815	1940	North Cascades
35. Thunder Peak	8,800+	1972	North Cascades
36. Oval Peak	8,795	unkn	North Cascades
37. Snow Dome	8,775	1953	North Cascades
38. Mt. Lago	8,745	1933	Okanogan
39. Robinson Mtn.	8,726	1904	Okanogan
40. Pandora's Box	8,720	1957	South Cascades
41. Colchuck Peak	8,705	1960	South Cascades
42. Star Peak	8,690	1898	North Cascades
43. Mt. Remmel	8,685	1904	North Cascades
44. Katsuk Peak	8,680	1968	North Cascades
45. Sahale Peak	8,680	1897	North Cascades
46. Fortress Mtn.	8,674	1962	North Cascades
47. Cannon Mtn.	8,638	unkn	South Cascades
48. Mt. Custer	8,630	1958	North Cascades
49. Ptarmigan Peak	8,614	unkn	North Cascades
50. Sherpa Peak	8,605	1955	South Cascades

(Compiled from Beckey, *Cascade Alpine Guides...*, copyright 1973, 1977 & 1981, The Mountaineers, reprinted with permission)

On summit of Columbia Crest, 1912. McGREGOR #72, COURTESY, THE MOUNTAINEERS

References

In the interest of space, I list here only the major books that have been of use in the making of this book—numerous other sources were consulted, including pamphlets, technical articles, historic documents and other books. The list below is intended to assist readers interested in further pursuing their own study of Washington's mountains by identifying the most useful and accessible sources among the veritable mountain of materials that comprise Washington's alpine literature.

Geology

Alt, David, and Donald W. Hyndman. *Roadside Geology of Washington.* Missoula: Mountain Press, 1984.

Crowder, D.F., and Rowland Tabor. *Routes and Rocks: Hiker's Guide to the North Cascades from Glacier Peak to Lake Chelan.* Seattle: The Mountaineers, 1965.

Easterbrook, Don, and David Rahm. *Landforms of Washington.* Bellingham: Western Washington State College, 1970.

Harris, Stephen. *Fire & Ice: The Cascade Volcanoes.* Revised ed. Seattle: The Mountaineers and Pacific Search Press, 1980.

McKee, Bates. *Cascadia: the Geologic Evolution of the Pacific Northwest.* New York: McGraw-Hill Book Company, 1972.

Mather, Kirtley, and Shirley Mason. *A Source Book in Geology.* Cambridge: Harvard University Press, 1939.

Sugden, David, and Brian S. John. *Glaciers and Landscape.* London: Edward Arnold, 1976.

Tabor, Rowland. *Guide to the Geology of Olympic National Park.* Seattle and London: University of Washington Press, 1975.

Tabor, Rowland, and D.F. Crowder. *Routes and Rocks in the Mt. Challenger Quadrangle.* Seattle: The Mountaineers, 1968.

Exploration & History

Judson, Phoebe Goodell. *Pioneer's Search for an Ideal Home.* Lincoln and London: University of Nebraska, 1984.

Paradise Inn, Mount Rainier National Park, no date. A. CURTIS #40475, WASHINGTON STATE HISTORICAL SOCIETY

Martinson, Arthur D. *Wilderness Above the Sound: the Story of Mt. Rainier National Park.* Flagstaff: Northland Press, 1986.

Meany, Edmond S. *Vancouver's Discovery of Puget Sound.* Portland: Binfords & Mort, 1957.

Miles, John C. *Koma Kulshan: The Story of Mt. Baker.* Seattle: The Mountaineers, 1984.

Roe, JoAnn. *The North Cascadians.* Seattle: Madrona Publishers, 1980.

Wagner, Henry R. *Spanish Explorations of the Strait of Juan de Fuca.* Santa Ana: Fine Arts Press, 1933.

Winthrop, Theodore. *Canoe and Saddle.* Nisqually ed. Portland: Binfords & Mort.

Wood, Robert. Men*, Mules and Mountains: Lieutenant O'Neil's Olympic Expeditions.* Seattle: The Mountaineers, 1976.

Lifeforms

Arno, Stephen, and Ramona P. Hammerly. *Northwest Trees.* Seattle: The Mountaineers, 1977.

Arno, Stephen. *Timberline: Mountain and Arctic Frontiers.* Seattle: Mountaineers, 1984.

Hitchcock, C. Leo, Arthur Cronquist, et al. *Vascular Plants of the Pacific Northwest—Parts I-V.* Seattle and London: University of Washington Press, 1969.

Larrison, Earl J. *Mammals of the Northwest.* Seattle: Seattle Audubon Society, 1976.

Mountaineering

Beckey, Fred. *Challenge of the North Cascades.* Seattle: Mountaineers, 1969.

Beckey, Fred. *Cascade Alpine Guide: Climbing and High Routes—Columbia River to Stevens Pass.* Seattle: The Mountaineers, 1973.

Beckey, Fred. *Cascade Alpine Guide: Climbing and High Routes—Stevens Pass to Rainy Pass.* Seattle: The Mountaineers, 1977.

Beckey, Fred. *Cascade Alpine Guide: Climbing and High Routes—Rainy Pass to Fraser River.* Seattle: The Mountaineers, 1981.

Coleman, Edmund T. "Mountaineering on the Pacific." *Harper's New Monthly Magazine* 39 (November 1869): 793-817.

Molenaar, Dee. *The Challenge of Rainier.* Seattle: The Mountaineers,1971.

Olympic Mountain Rescue. *Climber's Guide to the Olympic Mountains.* Seattle: Olympic Mountain Rescue and The Mountaineers, 1979.

Other Sources

The following agencies and organizations play active roles in the management, protection and thoughtful use of Washington's mountainscapes and their resources.

Agencies

National Park Service

North Cascades National Park
2105 Highway 20
Sedro Wooley, WA 98284

Mt. Rainier National Park
Tahoma Woods
Star Route
Ashford, WA 98304

Olympic National Park
600 East Park Avenue
Port Angeles, WA 98362

U.S. Forest Service

Mt. St. Helens National Volcanic Monument
Route 1, Box 369
Amboy, WA 98601

Gifford Pinchot National Forest
500 W. 12th Street
Vancouver, WA 98660

Mt. Baker-Snoqualmie National Forest
1022 First Avenue
Seattle, WA 98104

Wenatchee National Forest
301 Yakima Street
Wenatchee, WA 98801

Okanogan National Forest
1240 Second Avenue S.
Okanogan, WA 98840

Olympic National Forest
Federal Building
Olympia, WA 98507

Washington Department of Game
600 N. Capitol Way
Olympia, WA 98504

Washington Department of Natural Resources
John A. Cherberg Bldg.
Room 201
Olympia, WA 98504

U.S Geological Survey
Public Inquiries Office
Room 678
U.S. Courthouse
West 920 Riverside Ave.
Spokane, WA 99201

Organizations

The Mountaineers
300 3rd Avenue W.
Seattle, WA 98119

Mazamas
909 N.W. 19th Street
Portland, Or 97209

The Cascadians
P.O. Box 2201
Yakima, WA 98907

Spokane Mountaineers
P.O. Box 1013
Spokane, WA 99210

Sierra Club
1516 Melrose
Seattle, WA 98122

Washington Native Plant Society
Dept. of Botany, KB-15
University of Washington
Seattle, WA 98195

Coalition for Washington Wildlife
P.O. Box 1731
Seattle, WA 98111

On snow slope below Coleman Peak, Mt. Baker, no date. A. CURTIS #7436, WASHINGTON STATE HISTORICAL SOCIETY

Stevens Highway Pass, no date. PICKETT #4354, UNIVERSITY OF WASHINGTON LIBRARIES, SPECIAL COLLECTIONS DIVISION

Next in the Washington Geographic Series

PAT O'HARA

THE WASHINGTON COAST

The wild coast of northern Washington, the sandy-beach coast to the south and the "straits" coast—each is different in character, each has a unique biological regime, each its own history. This beautiful volume in the Washington Geographic Series thoroughly explores the ultimate edge that is a coast through its inhabitants—such as the whale, sea otter, the razor clam; through its first human residents and through history of shipwrecks and communities that keep a precarious foothold on the coast. Some 150 color photographs by the northwest's best landscape photographers will provide a private tour of the forces of geology, marine biology, shoreline ecology and weather and of the restless sea that shapes the coast.

ABOUT THE WASHINGTON GEOGRAPHIC SERIES

This series is your guide to enjoying and understanding Washington's places, people and landscapes.

Color photography of the unspoiled country of Washington illustrates every book, and each text is written especially for this series to help you explore, experience and learn about this fascinating state.

WRITE TO:
AMERICAN GEOGRAPHIC PUBLISHING
P.O. BOX 5630
HELENA, MT 59604
(406) 443-2842

Titles in production or planning are:

Washington's Columbia River
Puget Sound
Washington: A Geography
Washington Habitats

Order early: Pre-publication discounts are available.

Please send us suggestions for titles you would like to see and your comments about what you see in this volume.